BEGINNER'S
— GUIDE TO —
CROCHET

20 CROCHET PROJECTS FOR BEGINNERS

Sarah Shrimpton

D&C
David and Charles

www.stitchcraftcreate.co.uk

CONTENTS

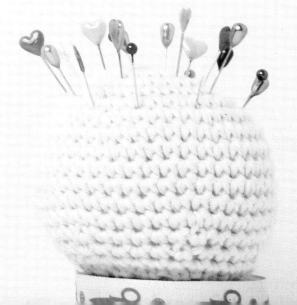

INTRODUCTION

So you've decided to learn to crochet? Excellent news! You'll love it, you really will. Crochet is good for the soul, the heart and the hands, and learning a new skill is great for the grey matter, too.

Once you can crochet, you will never again wonder what to do on a wet Saturday afternoon, or be bored on a lengthy car journey (as a passenger, I hasten to add!). Soon, crochet will become your constant companion as your spare moments are spent planning new projects and your home becomes filled with the wonderful things you have made. As for birthday and Christmas presents, you'll be hooking up beautiful handmade gifts in no time.

In fact, crochet can be used to make just about anything your creative heart desires. Want to make a cushion cover? What about a rug? How about a teddy bear, scarf, slippers, belt, poncho...? You know the answer, dear reader, crochet it.

What makes crochet so versatile is that it can be made in three different ways:

First, by hooking back and forth in rows to create flat pieces; these can be shaped and stitched together to construct something like a jumper or shawl.

Secondly, by working in rounds to produce circles; this is useful for rugs and coasters, but also important for starting many motifs, like granny squares, which can be joined together to make larger items, like blankets.

Thirdly, in three-dimensions; you work in rounds again but additional shaping can create spheres, sausage shapes, cones and cylinders, which can be used for toys, hats, bags and bowls.

All this with just a little hook and a length of yarn.

There's no messing around with circular hooks or cable hooks or double-pointed hooks here (yes, knitting, I'm talking about you). No, a standard hook is all you need to work in these three different ways. The reason for not needing lots of fancy-pants hooks is quite simple; in crochet, you only work with one stitch at a time and that is the one on your hook. There's no wrestling with hundreds of stitches on a stick and no cursing when you realize you've dropped one somewhere and the rest have slid off the stick and are now around your ankles (sorry, knitting, but I'm talking about you again). Crochet is altogether more forgiving, so even if you make a mistake (and we all do), it doesn't go and unravel itself all over the floor and you won't end up with gaping holes in the middle of your work.

To top all of this, did you know there are actually only a handful of stitches you need to learn to be competent at this super-yarny craft? It's what you do with them that can create something as simple as a dishcloth or as complicated as a doily.

So pull up a comfy chair, get yourself settled and I'll tell you everything you need to know.

Sarah x

P.S. I am not anti-knitting. I love knitting, and all knitty things. I really do.

P.P.S. You can actually get double-ended hooks, but that's an entirely different ball game and you won't need one for this book.

HOW TO USE THIS BOOK

Many crochet books follow a similar format; they have a section at the front explaining how to make all of the stitches, followed by the patterns, many of which combine several different stitches and techniques, not all of them suitable for a novice.

This book, however, is quite different. It has been carefully designed to teach you little by little. Who expects a crochet newbie to try learning all the stitches first and then attempt a complicated pattern? Not I. That would be madness!

No, we'll start at the very beginning and I'll show you what you need to have in your crochet kit. We'll have a little chat about patterns and charts before moving on to the exciting stuff, where you'll find out how to hold your hook and yarn and then you'll be ready to learn your first stitch. You'll need to have a little practise and once you're ready (it won't be long), you can tackle the accompanying project, which uses exactly what you have just learnt.

It makes sense, doesn't it? And you'll have made your very first piece of crochet on your very first day of learning! Hoorah!

The book continues in this way throughout; learn a new stitch or technique, practise, and then hone your new skills by making something with what you know. There are 20 wonderful projects to work through, which teach the basics of crocheting, along with other useful tips. The projects combine simple, modern design with a fairly quick outcome – some can be completed in less than an hour and most you should be able to finish in just a few hours. Each project details the yarn and hook I used to make the item, but of course you can choose your own and I'll tell you how to do that, too.

You'll be hooked in no time.

YOUR CROCHET TOOLKIT

Every craft needs a toolkit and crochet is no different. Apart from hooks and yarn, which will be covered on the next pages, some of the most useful things you'll need are:

SCISSORS

It goes without saying that you'll need to cut things when crocheting, yarn, threads, felt or material, and you'll need a decent pair of scissors for the task. Keep the kids away from them and they'll stay sharp (unlike mine, which are encrusted with glue and blunt as a spoon).

TAPESTRY/ DARNING NEEDLE

When you have completed your beautiful piece of crochet, you'll have yarn ends to get rid of. You can do this by simply sewing them into your work to hide them. Tapestry needles have a blunt end, so they don't catch on your stitches, and a large eye to thread the yarn through.

STITCH MARKER

When crocheting, you'll often want to identify an important stitch in your work. It might be the first stitch of a round, or a particularly tricky stitch to see. There are many designs available, but you can always use a piece of different coloured yarn and hook this through your stitch instead.

ROW COUNTER

This is useful for keeping track of how many rows or rounds you have completed. You can buy a traditional barrel-shaped counter, download an app or keep a tally with pen and paper.

SEWING NEEDLE

This is a sharp-ended needle and therefore perfect for attaching pretty things like ribbons and buttons to your work. It has a smaller eye as it will be used with cotton or embroidery threads.

THREAD

If you want to attach pretty things to your crochet, then you'll need some cotton thread. White and black are a staple in my kit, but you may want a few more colours for variety.

You may also like to embroider onto your crochet and if so, you'll want some embroidery threads in your stash, too.

TOY STUFFING

When making a plush item you'll need to fill it with something fluffy. Commercially produced toy stuffing is readily available and will add substance to your toys and cushions whilst conforming to all the proper safety guidelines.

SAFETY EYES

Not to be confused with safety goggles, safety eyes are the little plastic eyes used in toy making. You can, of course, embroider features onto your wonderful creation, but you may prefer to use safety eyes instead. Safety eyes are so called because they are pushed into your crochet and secured at the back with a tight-fitting washer, making them nigh on impossible to remove.

SPRAY STARCH

Sometimes your finished crochet piece can be a little floppy. Sometimes it doesn't matter, but sometimes it really does. If you've made a crochet snowflake to hang on your tree, then you'll want it to be crisp and pointy and spray starch can be used to block your work.

NON-RUST PINS

When crocheting, you'll need to pin things to keep them in place. You'll also need to pin out your crochet if you are blocking your work. The non-rust varieties are essential here so they don't leave nasty marks.

FELT AND FABRICS, RIBBONS AND BUTTONS

No crafter can ever have enough of these. Don't forget to raid your 'pile-of-stuff-to-be-thrown-out' and cut buttons from shirts and fabric from dresses. Crafty knick-knacks are in plentiful supply from high street haberdashers and online, so arm yourself with a treasure trove of pretties.

GLUE

Often it's easier to glue things to your crochet, rather than stitch them. The best for the job is a PVA-based glue, such as Tacky Glue, or something similar that will dry clear.

POMPOM MAKER

This useful little tool does exactly as the name suggests and is available in all manner of sizes to enable you to make some teeny tiny pompoms or the great big fluffy sort.

Now you just need to find somewhere to store your kit, away from sticky fingers and the cat, but I'll leave that up to you.

CHARM

YARN AND HOOKS

The world of yarn is a pretty big one and quite daunting to a beginner, but there are really only two things to consider: yarn weight (how thick it is) and yarn fibre (what it's made of). That's not too scary, is it?

YARN WEIGHT

Let's start with weight. It won't surprise you to know that yarn comes in a variety of thicknesses, from the very thin to the very thick. Examples are:

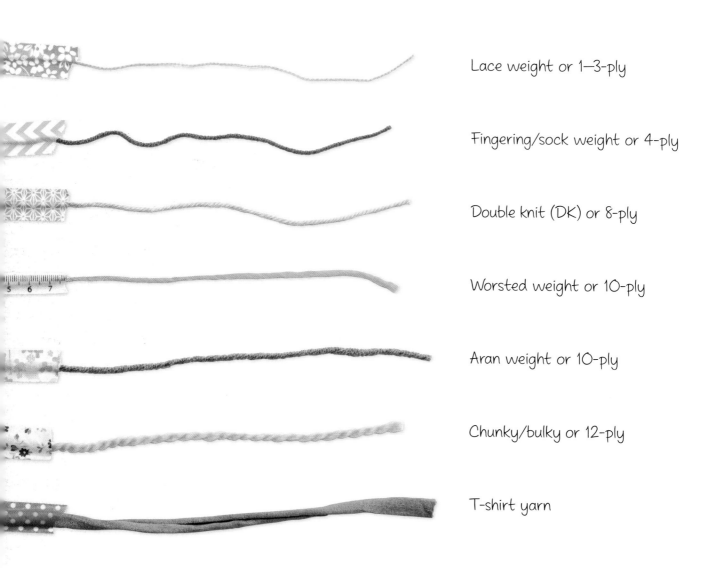

Lace weight or 1–3-ply

Fingering/sock weight or 4-ply

Double knit (DK) or 8-ply

Worsted weight or 10-ply

Aran weight or 10-ply

Chunky/bulky or 12-ply

T-shirt yarn

Which yarn to choose depends on what you're making; fine and lace weight yarns are perfect for crocheting delicate items like summer shawls, whilst the chunky-monkeys are great for winter woollies. T-shirt yarn, made of recycled selvedges from the textile industry, is substantial enough to make rugs and mats. And sock weight? I'll leave for you to work out yourself.

The weight of the yarn also determines the size of hook you will use; the finer the yarn, the thinner the hook, but more on that later.

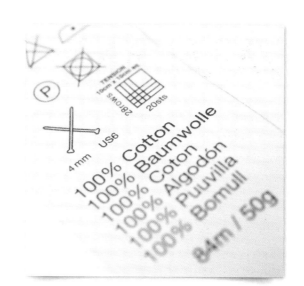

READING THE LABEL

When you buy yarn, it will be wound into a ball or skein often 25g, 50g or 100g and will have a label around it. This will identify the brand, the yarn name (there are some strange ones out there, I can tell you) and its weight. There will also be details of the fibre content, washing instructions and often a symbol of a pair of crossed needles, sometimes a hook, with recommended size. Other numbers indicate the colour and dye lot. Yarn is batch-dyed in lots, so this means that all of one dye-lot will be exactly the same shade. You'll want to buy enough yarn of the same dye-lot to complete your project, especially for large items using several balls of yarn.

YARN FIBRE

As yarn varies in weight, so it also differs in content. It can be made entirely of one material, or a combination of many. The main yarn fibre categories are synthetic, animal and plant and include:

Synthetic fibres

Acrylic and polyester yarns are made of synthetic fibres. They are strong, easy to care for and inexpensive, so work well for items subject to everyday rough and tumble, such as blankets, throws and cushions. Synthetic fibres are also used to make novelty yarns, such as those containing metallic threads or the extremely fluffy eyelash yarn.

Animal fibres

Wool, alpaca, mohair and silk yarns are luxurious, sometimes fluffy and often a bit more pricey. They have insulating properties, meaning that they are ideal for keeping you toasty-warm in cold weather.

Plant fibres

Cotton, bamboo and linen yarns are all non-allergenic and cooling, so are perfect for clothing, toys and baby accessories.

SUBSTITUTING YARN

Designers will usually suggest a specific yarn for their pattern, however, there are times when you'll want to find an alternative (you may prefer a different brand or the chosen yarn may be discontinued). In this case, you'll need to ensure that your replacement is the same weight and a similar fibre so that your finished crochet piece will be roughly the same size as the pattern states. That said, for some patterns, size or fibre doesn't matter and you can experiment with whatever yarn you please.

HOOKS

The word crochet comes from the French word, meaning 'hook' and after your yarn, is the next most important piece of your kit.

A standard hook is shorter than a knitting needle as you only work with one stitch on your hook at a time (apart from a few exceptions, but don't worry about them here). It is also shaped with a hook at one end (bet you didn't see that coming) and a flat bit (the grip), which is often stamped with the hook size.

Hooks differ in circumference to match the different yarn weights; from the needle-like 2.25mm (US 1/B), used with lace weight yarn, to the whopping 20mm (US 36), used with T-shirt yarn and other extreme yarns.

They are often made of aluminium or steel, but you can also find soft, ergonomically engineered hooks, as well as beautifully crafted bamboo ones. The larger hooks (12–20mm [US 17–36]) are usually made from plastic so they're not too heavy to work with.

Whilst some hooks have their size printed in millimetres on the shaft, many have a letter or number.

Choosing the right hook

This is actually very easy. First, the pattern will suggest a hook size to match the yarn specified. Secondly, check the label on the yarn (look for the crossed needles or hook symbol) but remember it is only a starting point for choosing the size; you may prefer working with a slightly smaller or larger hook than stated and that, dear reader, is fine.

It's also fun to play with the sizing in some patterns; why not take a delicate doily pattern and instead of using fine-weight cotton, use extreme yarn and an enormous hook? The result could be a very interesting rug.

The projects in this book require a variety of hook sizes so it's worth arming yourself with a good selection.

Conversion chart

This exciting chart shows you the conversions:

Note: this is only a guide. Actual sizes can vary by manufacturer.

MM	IMPERIAL	US
2	14	-
2.25	13	1/B
2.5	12	-
2.75	11	2/C
3	11	-
3.25	10	3/D
3.5	9	4/E
3.75	-	5/F
4	8	6/G
4.25	-	-
4.5	7	7
5	6	8/H
5.5	5	9/I
6	4	10/J
6.5	3	10.5/K
7	2	-
8	0	11/L
9	00	13/M/N
10	000	15/N/P
15	-	-
16	-	Q
19	-	35/S
20	-	36

PATTERNS AND CHARTS

Ok, so you've got a hook, some gorgeous yarn and a bag full of pretties. You're raring to go. What you need to do next is find a pattern and create something amazing. All you need to know about patterns is that you'll find them in two different formats — as written instructions or as a diagram made of symbols.

'YOU WILL NEED' LISTS

A written pattern is just like following a recipe. It has its own ingredients list, often imaginatively entitled 'you will need', which does indeed tell you what you need to complete the project. This covers the important things, like the yarn (brand, colour/shade number and quantity) and the hook you will need. It will also include any additional materials, such as felt, ribbons and toy stuffing. It may look like this:

YOU WILL NEED

- 4mm (US 6/G) hook
- 3 x 50g balls Rico Creative Cotton Aran in Turquoise (shade 36)
- Grey felt
- 2 x 9mm (⅜in) safety eyes

PATTERNS

Next in a written pattern are the instructions themselves and, just like a recipe, they'll describe each step you need to follow. They will be numbered and contain the information on stitch making for that specific row or round. They also use abbreviations.

It may look like this:

Row 3: Dc 7, dc2tog (8 sts)

Now to a beginner, this will look like gobbledygook. Don't worry; it will all make sense as you work through the book. For now, all you need to know is that these are the stitches made in Row 3.

ABBREVIATIONS

Written patterns usually abbreviate crochet terms to make them easier to read and will often supply a key. You'll soon get used to working from them and below are the main ones you will find.

Back loops only	BLO
Chain	ch
Double crochet	dc
Double crochet decrease	dc2tog
Half treble	htr
Right side	RS
Skip	sk
Slip stitch	sl st
Stitches	sts
Treble	tr
Wrong side	WS

UK—US crochet terminology

Crochet patterns can be written with UK or US terms. This means that some of the stitches have a slightly different name. It's nothing to worry about and the differences are shown below:

UK	US
Double crochet (dc)	Single crochet (sc)
Treble crochet (tr)	Double crochet (dc)
Half-treble crochet (htr)	Half-double crochet (hdc)
Double treble crochet (dtr)	Triple crochet (trc)

All of the patterns in this book are written using UK terms.

CHARTS

The other format for crochet patterns is a chart. This is quite simply a visual representation of the pattern, using symbols to depict the stitches, rather than words. Each row or round is marked with a number, so you know where you're heading. Throughout this book there will be examples of charts for you to see and work with.

The great thing about charts is that the symbols are standardized. Here are the main ones:

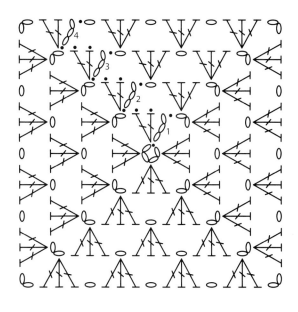

⬭	Chain		picot
•	Slip stitch		2 tr in same stitch
+	Double crochet		3 tr group
⊤	Treble crochet		4 tr shell
⊤	Half-treble crochet		5 tr shell
⋁	2dc in same stitch		7 tr shell
⋀	Dc2tog		2 tr cluster
⬭	5tr bobble cluster		3 tr cluster

MAKING UP

The final part of a written pattern will give instructions for how to make up or finish your project. It may tell you how to attach pieces, or what to sew to where.

I know that it all seems a little baffling at the moment, but let me assure you that this book is going to guide you through every step. Soon you'll be reading patterns and charts like a pro.

GET READY

Use whatever yarn and matching hook you have to hand to practise with, but I would recommend a 4mm (US 6/G) hook and some acrylic double knit yarn, many of the first projects in this book use these. If you find it a bit tricky to see what you're doing, then you could try some acrylic chunky and a 6mm (US 10/J) hook.

MAKING A SLIP KNOT

Whenever you crochet in rows, you'll need to begin with a slip knot. The tail of this knot can be pulled and tightened to secure the yarn to the hook.

1. First, make a loop with the yarn.

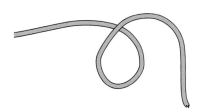

2. With your right hand, grab the middle part of the yarn tail and begin to pull it through the starting loop.

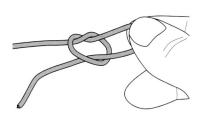

3. Hold both ends of the yarn with your left hand and use your right hand to pull the loop and tighten the knot.

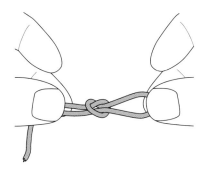

4. Put this loop onto your hook and tighten it by pulling the yarn tail. The knot (and all other stitches you make) should sit on the thickest part of the hook, called the shaft, just after the hook end.

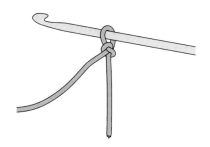

HOLDING YOUR HOOK

Know this: there is not a right or wrong way to do it. The important thing to know is that your right hand controls the hook, and it is the hook that makes the stitches by creating loops with the yarn.

There are two main positions for holding your hook. Try both and see what feels the most natural.

THE KNIFE HOLD

In your right hand, hold the hook with your hand over the top, thumb on one side and fingers on the other side of the grip.

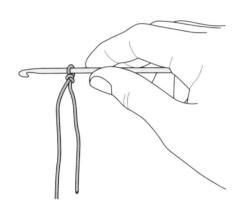

THE PEN HOLD

In your right hand, hold the hook as you would do a pen. Again, with your thumb and fingers on the grip.

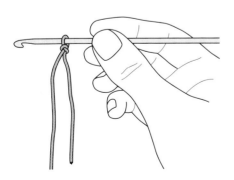

HOLDING THE YARN

There are a bazillion different ways to hold the yarn, the main thing to remember is that your left hand is for feeding and controlling the yarn.

Try this method to start with:

1. Feed the working part of the yarn around your little finger, and up and over your forefinger. Your little finger and forefinger control the flow of the yarn.

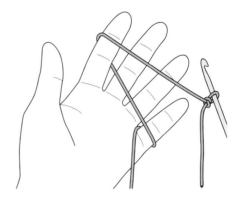

2. With your thumb and third finger, hold the yarn on the hook. This keeps everything in place.

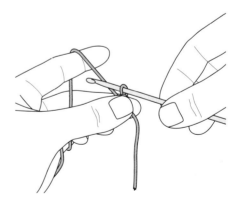

3. Steady the hook with your right hand.

And that, my friend, is a basic hold. Right, don't move. Just kidding.

Try it all again a few times. To begin with, it will feel mighty strange and awkward. But with practise it will become more comfortable and your movements will happen naturally. In no time at all you'll have developed your own style which suits you.

Ready? Then let's get started...

START
STITCHING

Now you know how to hold your yarn and hook, it's time to get crocheting and this chapter covers the basic stitches (I meant it when I said there's only a handful you need to learn). So, you'll meet chain stitch, double crochet stitch, treble stitch and half-treble stitch – I'll show you how to make them and get you working on some gorgeous projects, too.

Remember that you are learning a new skill and don't be disheartened if everything goes pear-shaped to start with. You are a beginner. Practise is all you need.

(You should see some of my disastrous first attempts...)

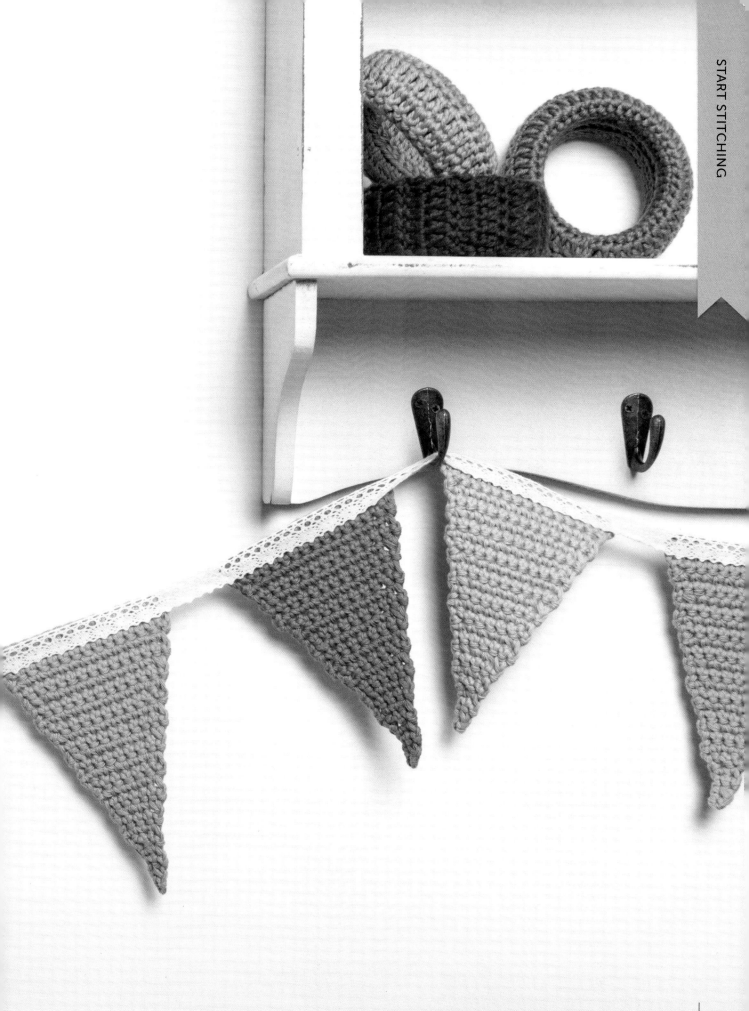

CHAIN STITCH

A chain of stitches is a very useful thing and can be as long or short as required. When working in rows it provides the foundation of your piece, and in decorative work it can produce shapes and spaces. In a pattern, chain is written 'ch', so a chain of five stitches would be written 'ch5'.

The first projects in this book are based on working in rows, so you'll need to make a foundation chain to begin them.

CHART

In a diagram, chain stitches look like this.

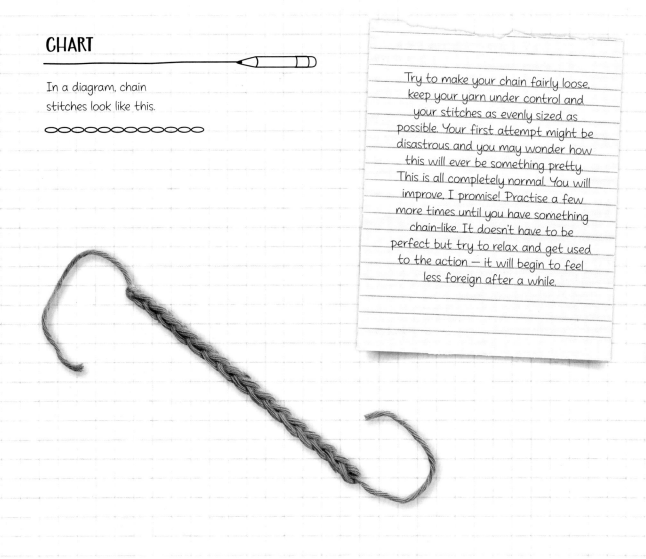

Try to make your chain fairly loose, keep your yarn under control and your stitches as evenly sized as possible. Your first attempt might be disastrous and you may wonder how this will ever be something pretty. This is all completely normal. You will improve, I promise! Practise a few more times until you have something chain-like. It doesn't have to be perfect but try to relax and get used to the action — it will begin to feel less foreign after a while.

HOW TO CHAIN STITCH

1. Okay, grab your practise yarn and hook, make a slip knot with the yarn and secure it on your hook (see Making a slip knot).

2. Now twist your hook anti-clockwise so that the yarn is over your hook. This move is known as 'yarn over'.

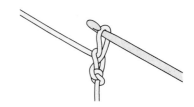

3. Catch the yarn with the hook and pull it through the loop already on your hook. Ch 1 made. Continue in the same way to make a chain of 15 stitches (ch 15).

Counting your stitches

Each crochet stitch produces a 'V' shape at the top. The 'V' is made of two loops: the front loop (the one nearest you) and the back loop (the one furthest away). When you count your stitches, you should never include the loop on your hook as that's the next stitch waiting to happen.

Turning chain

When working in rows, you need to make an extra chain at the beginning of each row. This is called a 'turning chain' and it helps you reach up to the next row by mimicking the height of the stitch you are using; a double crochet needs a turning chain of just one.

Back of the chain

Just so you know – this is the back of the chain. Those little ridges are called the 'butt' of the stitch.

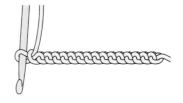

WORKING INTO THE CHAIN

There are three different methods for you to try:

DIFFICULT

Insert your hook through both loops of the 'V' and between the 'butt'. It gives a nice finish, but it's a bit of an awkward manoeuvre and may test your patience.

MEDIUM-LY TRICKY

Insert your hook under the top loop of the 'V' and the 'butt', leaving the bottom loop free. This gives a tidy edge and is slightly less tricky than the first option.

EASY PEASY

Why bother with all the faffing around when you can just insert your hook under the top loop and be done with it? The finish can be a little gappy, but honestly, as a beginner, let's keep it simple.

DOUBLE CROCHET

Double crochet is a short, chunky little stitch that produces a dense, solid material without much stretch. It's referred to as 'dc' in written patterns.

CHART

Start with the row at the very bottom, reading from left to right. This isn't numbered because it's the foundation row. Here, it contains 15 chain stitches. Row 1 runs from right to left and shows the turning chain, followed by 15 double crochet stitches. Row 2 reads from left to right again with the next turning chain and another row of double crochet stitches.

Don't worry about making mistakes. It's very easy to end up with more or fewer stitches than you started with and happens to even the most experienced crocheter. Crochet behaves itself nicely and doesn't unravel all over the floor. That is what makes it so easy to correct any problems. Just remove your hook and gently pull back the yarn to where the mistake is, or the beginning of a row, if that's easier. Then re-insert your hook into the working loop and off you go again...

Remember to make a turning chain at the beginning of every row and then ignore it, inserting your hook into the second stitch from your hook each time.

Foundation chain: make a foundation chain of 15

First, you'll need a foundation chain of 15 (see Stitch tutorial: Chain Stitch).

Row 1: (ch 1) dc 15 (15 sts)

1. Chain one (turning chain) and then work back along the foundation chain just made. Working from right to left, insert your hook in the second chain from the hook (ignore the turning chain).

2. Yarn over hook, and pull the yarn through the stitch. ('The stitch' refers to the stitch you have just inserted your hook into. In this illustration, it's the first loop on the hook).

3. You will have two loops on your hook. Yarn over again. Now pull the yarn through both loops on your hook.

4. Double crochet stitch made. Hooray!

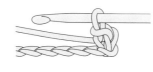

5. Repeat this process across your chain, right up to the slip knot. You should have 15 double crochet stitches (see Counting your stitches).

When you crochet in rows, your work will seem the same on both sides. However, if you look really closely, you'll see a difference between the front and the back of the stitches:

Row 2: (ch 1, turn) dc 15 (15 sts)

From now on, it gets much easier; when you work back through this, and all the other rows of stitches, you must work through both loops of the 'V'.

1. Chain one (your turning chain) and then turn the work, making the double crochet stitches in exactly the same way.

2. Starting in the second stitch from your hook (ignore the turning chain), insert the hook through both loops (the 'V') of the stitch.

3. Yarn over hook and pull the yarn through the stitch (you should have two loops on the hook).

4. Yarn over again, this time pulling the yarn through both loops. Double crochet made!

5. Continue across the row, remembering to insert your hook through both loops of the 'V' and count your stitches at the end.

Row 3: Continue as per Row 2 from now on.

COSY CAFETIÈRE

This cafetière cosy is a perfect first project — there are no surprises here. You will practise making a slip knot, chain and double crochet stitches and this is your first chance to work from a very simple crochet pattern.

YOU WILL NEED

I have used...

- 1 x 100g ball Rowan Pure Wool Aran in Cedar (shade 674)

You could use...

- Any yarn and hook to match, any Aran weight yarn with some wool content for insulation will work

You will also need...

- A cafetière
- 4.5mm (US 7) hook
- Tapestry needle
- 90cm (35½in) length of ribbon, 3mm (⅛in) wide and cut into 30cm (12in) lengths

Finished size:

28 x 14cm (11 x 5½in)

PATTERN

At the beginning of every row, remember to chain one and turn. This is important as a pattern will often state this at the top, rather than print it on every row.

Foundation chain: ch 50 (quite loosely)
Row 1: dc 50 across the chain (starting in the 2nd stitch from hook)
Rows 2–30: dc 50 (starting in 2nd stitch from hook)
Fasten off (see Fastening off). Weave in ends (see Weaving in ends).

MAKING UP

To add the ribbon ties, thread the ribbon through your tapestry needle and sew it in between the stitches from one side to the other. You might find it easier to put the cosy around your cafetière first. Tie the ribbon into a bow and tadaaaaaah! Your very first piece of crochet is made.

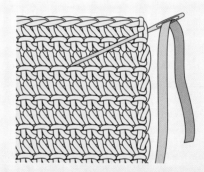

Adjusting the pattern

You can easily adjust this pattern for your cafetière by measuring the circumference. Your starting chain will need to measure 2cm (¾in) less. To adjust the height of your cosy, just make more or fewer rows.

DOUBLE CROCHET DECREASE

Unless you are happy making rectangles forever, then you'll need to know how to change the number of stitches in your row. To decrease stitches, a common method is to double crochet two stitches together, abbreviated as 'dc2tog' in patterns.

CHART

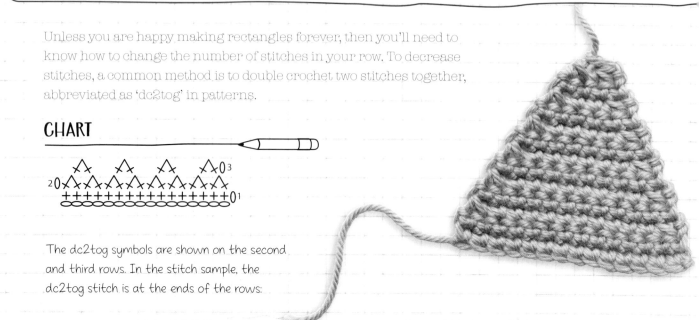

The dc2tog symbols are shown on the second and third rows. In the stitch sample, the dc2tog stitch is at the ends of the rows:

Foundation chain: Make a foundation chain of 16.

Row 1: (ch 1) dc 16

1. For this row, make 16 double crochet stitches as before. Remember to make the turning chain at the beginning.

Row 2: (ch 1, turn) dc2tog to end (8 sts)

1. Chain one and turn. To make the decrease, insert your hook into the second stitch from your hook, under both strands of the 'V'.

2. Yarn over hook and pull yarn through the stitch (you will have two loops on your hook). Now insert your hook into the next stitch (see arrow).

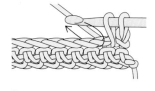

3. Yarn over hook and pull yarn through the stitch (now with three loops on your hook). Yarn over hook again and pull yarn through all three loops.

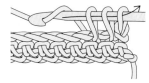

4. Now, continue across your work, decreasing the stitches as you go. At the end of the row you will have eight stitches – shown as '(8 sts)' in the pattern.

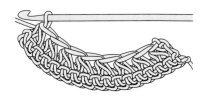

Row 3: (ch 1, turn) dc2tog to end (4 sts)

1. Chain one, turn and decrease (dc2tog) across to the end of the row.

Once you feel confident you are ready to try the Bye-Baby-Bunting project (see Bye-Baby-Bunting).

STITCH TUTORIAL:

DOUBLE CROCHET INCREASE

The next step is to learn how to increase stitches in your work. This is another way to shape your work and it couldn't be easier, all you do is add more than one stitch into the stitch you are working on. An increase will be shown as '2dc in next st' or something similar, depending on the pattern.

CHART

In the sample, the increases are at the ends of the rows:

Foundation chain: ch 8

Row 1: (ch 1) dc 8

Row 2: (ch 1, turn) 2dc in each st to end (16 sts)

1. It's very simple to make two double crochet into a single stitch. Make the double crochet as you usually would then put another one in exactly the same stitch (see arrow).

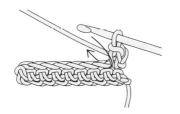

2. In every stitch make two double crochet. You will end up with 16 stitches at the end of the row.

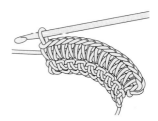

Row 3: (ch 1, turn) (dc 1, 2dc in next st) repeat to end (24 sts)

1. Now this is a bit different. Here, you need to make one double crochet in the first stitch of the row, then two double crochet into the next stitch, alternating between one double crochet and two double crochet across the row. You'll end up with 24 stitches at the end.

Keep practising until you feel confident. Once you think you're ready, the Little Hearts project (see Little Hearts) awaits you...it's a bit more of a challenge, with a couple of new techniques thrown into the mix, but you are more than ready.

BYE-BABY-BUNTING

These pretty bunting flags are made by crocheting back and forth in rows of double crochet. A simple dc2tog decrease is made at the beginning and end of every third row to shape the work into a triangle.

YOU WILL NEED

I have used...

• 1 x 50g ball Drops Paris Cotton Aran in: Light Purple (shade 05), Medium Purple (shade 31), Light Blue Purple (shade 32), Light Light Pink (shade 57), Powder Pink (shade 58), Light Old Pink (shade 59), Dark Old Pink (shade 60)

You could use...

• Yarn and hook to match

You will also need...

• 4.5mm (US 7) hook
• Tapestry needle
• 3m (3½ yd) of lace ribbon
• Sewing needle and thread and/or a PVA-based glue
• Spray starch

Finished size:

9 x 13cm (3½ x 5in).

PATTERN

(Make 19)

Foundation chain: ch 16
At the beginning of every row, chain 1 and turn.

Row 1: dc 16
Row 2: dc 16
Row 3: dc2tog, dc 12, dc2tog (14 sts)
Row 4: dc 14
Row 5: dc 14
Row 6: dc2tog, dc 10, dc2tog (12 sts)
Row 7: dc 12
Row 8: dc 12
Row 9: dc2tog, dc 8, dc2tog (10 sts)
Row 10: dc 10
Row 11: dc 10
Row 12: dc2tog, dc 6, dc2tog (8 sts)
Row 13: dc 8
Row 14: dc 8
Row 15: dc2tog, dc 4, dc2tog (6 sts)
Row 16: dc 6
Row 17: dc 6
Row 18: dc2tog, dc 2, dc2tog (4 sts)
Row 19: dc 4
Row 20: dc 4
Row 21: dc2tog, dc2tog (2 sts)
Row 22: dc 2
Row 23: dc 2
Row 24: dc2tog (1 st)
Row 25: dc 1
Fasten off (see Fastening off). Weave in ends (see Weaving in ends).

A word of caution about the yarn: I chose it because I love the colours, but it does have a tendency to split. However, it's easily substituted for another yarn, without altering the pattern.

MAKING UP

Block your triangles (see Finishing touches), once they're dry sew or glue the ribbon along the tops of the flags, leave around 25cm (10in) of ribbon at the beginning and end for hanging and a gap of 3cm (1¼in) between each flag. Next, hang your bunting for all to enjoy!

Troubleshooting

As you are working, your triangles may curl, and curly bunting flags are a definite no-no, you can use spray starch to help it keep its shape.

CHART

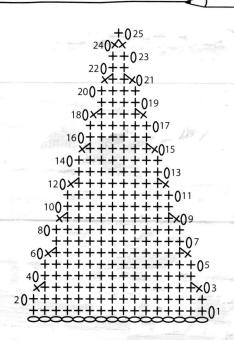

LITTLE HEARTS

These sweet little hearts are crocheted in rows of double crochet, using increases and decreases at the ends of the rows to shape them. Instead of sewing the two pieces together, I'll show you how to join them using double crochet. They're so simple, it's stopping making them you might have trouble with!

YOU WILL NEED

I have used...

• 1 x 100g ball Stylecraft Classic Cotton DK in: Teal (shade 3566), Soft Lime (shade 3663), Nocturne (shade 3669), Azure (shade 3671), Shrimp (shade 3674), Silver (shade 3675), Tropical Jade (shade 3676)
• 1 x 50g ball Rico Creative Cotton Aran in Vanilla (shade 62)

You could use...

• Yarn and hook to match

You will also need...

• 4mm (US 6/G) hook
• Tapestry needle
• Toy stuffing
• Ribbons, string and buttons to decorate

Finished size

Large heart 11 x 9cm (4½ x 3½in)
Small heart 8 x 7cm (3¼ x 2¾ in)

SMALL HEART

CHART

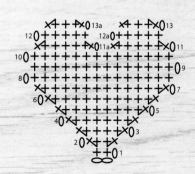

PATTERN

(Make 2)

Foundation chain: ch 2
At the beginning of every row, chain one and turn.

Row 1: dc 2
Row 2: 2dc in each st (4 sts)
Row 3: 2dc in first st, dc 2, 2dc in last st (6 sts)
Row 4: 2dc in first st, dc 4, 2dc in last st (8 sts)
Row 5: 2dc in first st, dc 6, 2dc in last st (10 sts)
Row 6: 2dc in first st, dc 8, 2dc in last st (12 sts)
Row 7: 2dc in first st, dc 10, 2dc in last st (14 sts)
Rows 8–10: dc 14

Rows 11–13 of the pattern shape one half of the top of the heart. This means that in row 11, only the first seven stitches are worked before turning and continuing back across for row 12.

Row 11: dc2tog, dc 3, dc2tog (5 sts)
Row 12: dc 5
Row 13: dc2tog, dc 1, dc2tog (3 sts)
Fasten off (see Fastening off).

There's no need to turn the heart so just put a slip knot on your hook and insert it into the seventh stitch from the left on row 10.

Row 11a: dc2tog, dc 3, dc2tog (5 sts)
Row 12a: dc 5
Row 13a: dc2tog, dc 1, dc2tog (3 sts)
Fasten off.

MAKING UP

To join your two sides together, place one on top of the other, ensuring both pieces are the same way around. There is no exact science to this, but you'll soon get the hang of it:

1. Starting at the bottom of the heart, put a slip knot on your hook and insert your hook through a stitch near the edge of both of the heart pieces. Yarn over and make a double crochet.

2. Continue to make double crochet stitches through the stitches at the very edge of both of the hearts and crochet around in an anti-clockwise direction. You may need to put two or more double crochet stitches in some of the stitches around the top of the heart to even out the shape.

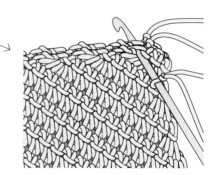

3. Before getting back to where you started, stuff the heart with the toy stuffing. Then finish making double crochet stitches to the end and fasten off. Weave in the ends (see Weaving in ends).

4. To complete your heart, decorate however you like, adding ribbons to hang them or buttons to embellish.

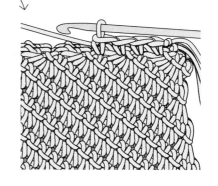

You can poke any yarn tails inside the heart as you work, that way there'll be no need to weave them in later.

LARGE HEART

CHART

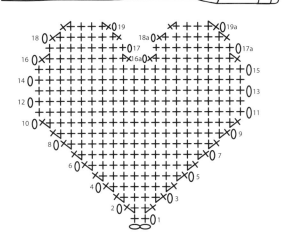

PATTERN

(Make 2)

Foundation chain: ch 2
At the beginning of every row, chain one and turn.

Row 1: dc 2
Row 2: 2dc in each st (4 sts)
Row 3: 2dc in first st, dc 2, 2dc in last st (6 sts)
Row 4: 2dc in first st, dc 4, 2dc in last st (8 sts)
Row 5: 2dc in first st, dc 6, 2dc in last st (10 sts)
Row 6: 2dc in first st, dc 8, 2dc in last st (12 sts)
Row 7: 2dc in first st, dc 10, 2dc in last st (14 sts)
Row 8: 2dc in first st, dc 12, 2dc in last st (16 sts)
Row 9: 2dc in first st, dc 14, 2dc in last st (18 sts)
Row 10: 2dc in first st, dc 16, 2dc in last st (20 sts)
Rows 11–15: dc 20

Rows 16–19 shape half of the top of the heart. So, in row 16, only work the first 10 stitches before turning and continuing back across for row 17.

Row 16: dc2tog, dc 6, dc2tog (8 sts)
Row 17: dc 8
Row 18: dc2tog, dc 4, dc2tog (6 sts)
Row 19: dc2tog, dc 2, dc2tog (4 sts)
Fasten off.

Turn your heart and put a slip knot on your hook and insert it into the tenth stitch from the left on row 15.

Row 16a: dc2tog, dc 6, dc2tog (8 sts)
Row 17a: dc 8
Row 18a: dc2tog, dc 4, dc2tog (6 sts)
Row 19a: dc2tog, dc 2, dc2tog (4 sts)
Fasten off.

MAKING UP

To finish, double crochet the two heart pieces together in the same way as the small heart.

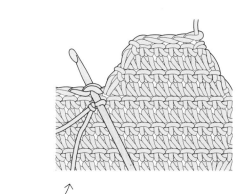

STITCH TUTORIAL:
TREBLE CROCHET

Treble crochet is slightly taller than double crochet. This is achieved by wrapping the yarn around your hook before you even begin making the stitch. Trebles are useful for adding height to your work and are important in making decorative motifs. They also have a bit more stretch than their chunky little cousin, double crochet. Treble crochet will be shown as 'tr' in a pattern.

As with double crochet, you need to remember to make a turning chain, however, because treble stitch is taller one chain stitch will not be enough, you will need to make a turning chain of three stitches to match the height of a treble stitch.

CHART

This is what the treble stitch looks like worked in rows:

This is the crochet chart for the treble stitch. Here, you can see that the three turning chain stitches count as a treble stitch:

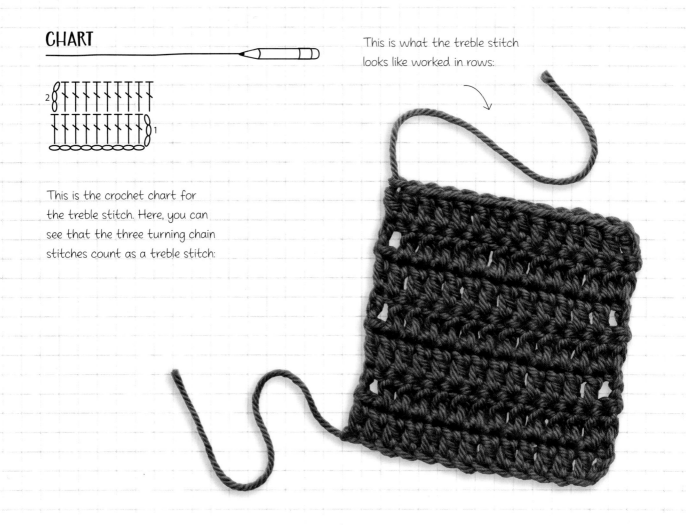

Foundation chain: ch 9

Row 1: (ch 3) tr 9 (10 sts)

1. So for Row 1 you need to chain three more stitches (additional to your foundation chain) for the turning chain, then work back along the foundation chain.

2. To make the treble stitch, yarn over and insert your hook into the fourth chain from your hook (ignore the first three chains as that is the turning chain).

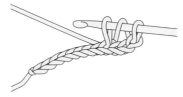

3. Yarn over and pull the yarn through the stitch, you should have three loops on your hook.

4. Next, yarn over and pull the yarn through the first two loops on your hook, leaving you with two loops on your hook.

5. To finish the treble stitch, yarn over and pull the yarn through the remaining two loops. Treble crochet stitch made!

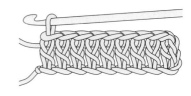

6. Continue along the row, remembering to wrap the yarn over your hook before you make each stitch. When you reach the end you will have nine treble stitches and one chain of three stitches. The turning chain counts as a treble stitch, so in fact you have 10 stitches.

Row 2: (ch 3, turn) tr 9 (10 sts)

1. For the next row, chain three (the turning chain), and turn your work.

2. Yarn over and insert your hook into the fifth stitch from your hook. Ignore the turning chain and the stitch at the base of that (if you crochet into here, you'll add an extra stitch to every row). So, treble crochet in the fifth stitch and continue until you reach the turning chain from the row below.

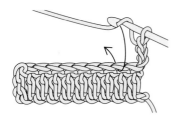

3. The turning chain, you remember is acting as a stitch, so make your last treble stitch in the top stitch of the chain.

4. At the end of the row, you will have 10 stitches (nine 'real' trebles and one chain-of-three-pretending-to-be-a-treble). Job done.

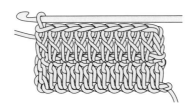

Continue to practise along the rows, remembering the turning chain of three. Once you've got the hang of it, then you're ready for the next project.

UPCYCLED BRACELETS

Do you have a chunky bracelet you're bored with? Not anymore! With a little crochet, some glue and a needle, you can bring it right up to date. This is a quick and easy project for you to practise treble stitch. This pattern is easily adjustable to fit any size bracelet (see Adjusting the pattern).

YOU WILL NEED

I have used...
- 1 x 50g ball Rowan Handknit Cotton DK in: Slate (shade 347), Aubergine (shade 348) and Seafoam (shade 352)

You could use...
- Any yarn and hook to match

You will also need...
- A bracelet
- 4mm (US 6/G) hook
- Tapestry needle
- PVA-based glue

Finished size:
26 x 7cm (10¼ x 2¾in)

AUBERGINE BRACELET

PATTERN

Foundation chain: ch 12
Row 1: (ch 3) tr 12 (starting in 4th chain from hook) (13 sts)
Rows 2–24: (ch 3, turn) tr 12 (starting in 5th chain from hook) (13 sts)
Fasten off (see Fastening off), leaving a 1m (40in) tail for making up.

Adjusting the pattern

You can easily adjust this pattern to match any bracelet you want to re-vamp. Just measure around the width of the bracelet and make your starting chain the same measurement.

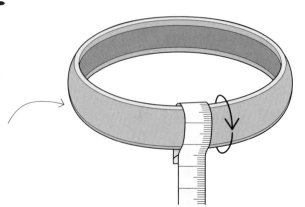

GREY AND GREEN BRACELETS

PATTERN

Foundation chain: ch 44
Row 1: (ch 3) tr 44 (starting in 4th chain from hook) (45 sts)
Rows 2–6: (ch 3, turn) tr 44 (starting in 5th chain from hook) (45 sts)
Fasten off, leaving a 1m (40in) tail for making up.

Adjusting the pattern

Measure the circumference and make your starting chain five stitches less than this measurement.

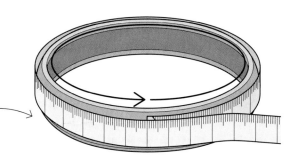

Remember to chain three and begin your first row in the fourth chain from your hook. Then, for all future rows, chain three, turn and begin in the fifth chain from your hook. Make enough rows to fit around your bracelet, checking the fit regularly.

MAKING UP

1. This is oh, so easy. First, make sure your crochet fits the bracelet and add some dabs of glue around the outside edge.

2. Wrap your crochet around the bracelet with the glue holding it in place, thread your tapestry needle with the long tail and sew the short sides together on the outside.

3. Once this is done, you just need to stitch the long edges together on the inside of the bracelet. There really is no special technique for doing this and because it's on the inside it won't be visible — so just freestyle. Thread your tapestry needle through the stitches to make a robust join between the two edges, you can also add dabs of glue as you go to stick it in place, too.

4. Fasten off the ends and allow to dry before wearing and showing off.

OTHER THINGS TO TRY

This is another great little project for using up leftover yarn. You could alternate between rows of double crochet and treble crochet for a nice variation, and more practise too! Just remember to use the correct length turning chain for the different stitches.

HALF-TREBLE CROCHET

The half-treble stitch is exactly that, half of a treble stitch! It's a teeny bit taller than a double crochet and smaller than a treble. Like double crochet, the half-treble creates a fairly dense stitch, but with a bit more stretch. A half-treble stitch is abbreviated as 'htr' in pattern speak.

To begin with, a half-treble is made in the same way as a treble and it too needs a turning chain, this time of just two stitches. When working in rows of half-trebles the turning chain doesn't count as a stitch. So, you'll be pleased to hear there are no fiddly stitches in the top of the chains.

CHART

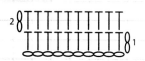

The half-treble symbol used in the chart is similar to the treble. You can see that the two turning chains are ignored at the beginning of each row.

Foundation chain: ch 10

Row 1: (ch 2) htr 10 (10 sts)

1. Chain two, work back along the foundation chain and wrap the yarn over your hook. Insert the hook into the third stitch from the hook, ignoring the two chain stitches from your turning chain.

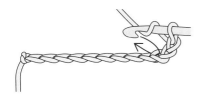

2. Yarn over and pull the yarn through the stitch, you should have three loops on your hook.

3. Yarn over and pull through all the loops. That's your half-treble stitch made!

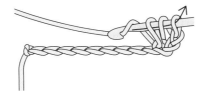

4. Repeat this across the chain.

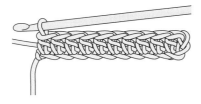

Row 2: (ch 2, turn) htr 10 (10 sts)

1. Chain two, turn and repeat as before, making your first half-treble into the third stitch from your hook each time.

Practise a few more rows and get ready for the project. There's going to be lots and lots of half-trebles in this one!

It can sometimes be a little fiddly to pull the yarn through all three loops when making the half-treble stitch, so keep the yarn fairly loose and try rolling your hook from side to side to encourage the loops to loosen for you.

SIMPLE DISHCLOTHS

I hate housework but give me a cheery dishcloth and the job suddenly seems appealing. Crocheted in rows of half-treble and edged with a contrasting double crochet stitch in sturdy cotton yarn, these dishcloths would also make great flannels, dusters and general wiper-downers. And as they're made in sturdy cotton yarn, they're machine-washable and will last for years.

YOU WILL NEED

I have used...

- 1 x 50g ball Rico Creative Cotton Aran in:

  A) Mouse Grey (shade 28)

  B) White (shade 80)

  C) Pistachio (shade 44)

  D) Turquoise (shade 36)

You could use...

- Any yarn and hook to match – 100% cotton double knit or kitchen cotton will work well

You will also need...

- 4mm (US 6/G) hook
- Tapestry needle

Finished size:

large dishcloth
20 x 20cm (8 x 8in)
small dishcloth
15 x 15cm (6 x 6in)

LARGE DISHCLOTH

PATTERN

At the beginning of each row, you need to chain two but remember, this turning chain does not count as a stitch when making half-trebles. After Row 1, turn your work after each turning chain.

Foundation chain: using colour A, ch 35
Row 1–26: htr 35
Fasten off (see Fastening off) and weave in the ends (see Weaving in ends).

Edging

This is your first colour change but don't worry, it's easy to do for this project. Attach the white yarn onto your hook with a slip knot (see Making a slip knot).

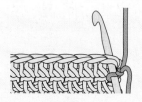

Now just thread your hook through one of the half-treble stitches — you can start anywhere, but I like to start about three stitches in from a corner — and just begin your double crochet stitch. Remember to work from right to left, in an anticlockwise direction.

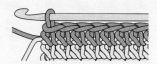

You'll find that the sides to your dishcloth have fewer stitches than the top and bottom edges. This is because the half-treble stitch is taller than it is wide. Don't worry if you end up with more or less stitches than the edging pattern states, it really doesn't matter.

Round 1: using colour B, *dc 33 along top/bottom edge, 3dc into corner stitch, dc 24 along side edge, 3dc into corner stitch.* * repeat on each side of dishcloth. Fasten off.

Round 2: using colour C, *dc 35 along top/bottom edge, 2dc into corner stitch, dc 26 along side edge, 2dc into corner stitch.* *repeat on each side of dishcloth. Fasten off and weave in the ends.

SMALL DISHCLOTH

PATTERN

You need to chain two at the beginning of each row, but don't count the turning chain as a stitch. After Row 1, turn your work after each turning chain.

Foundation chain: using colour C or D, ch 25
Row 1–19: htr 25
Fasten off and weave in ends.

Edging

As with the large dishcloth, attach the white yarn to your hook with a slip knot, thread through a stitch on the outside edge of your small dishcloth and double crochet around the edge.

Round 1: using colour B, *dc 23 along top/bottom edge, 3dc into corner stitch, dc 17 along side edge, 3dc into corner stitch.* * repeat on each side of dishcloth. Fasten off.

Round 2: using colour C, *dc 25 along top/bottom edge, 2dc into corner stitch, dc 19 along side edge, 2dc into corner stitch.* *repeat on each side of dishcloth. Fasten off and weave in the ends.

OTHER THINGS TRY

These dishcloths are great — practical and pretty! You could try adding a hanging loop by sewing a length of ribbon to a corner for easy storage. Varying the colours to match with your décor would be a nice touch, and if you're feeling really daring you could alternate between rows of half-treble stitch and double crochet for a nice textured version.

PICK 'N' STITCH

Alrighty clever clogs, you already know how to make the basic stitches so it's about time to mix it up a little. Whilst crocheting in one stitch can be very effective, and certainly has its uses, plenty of patterns call for you to use a whole load of different stitches – it might be that you'll change stitch every row, or within a row you'll need to make different combinations.

Using a variety of stitches can create some amazing effects and make for some wonderful patterns across your work. Often you'll skip stitches and use chain stitches to create spaces. You might also find tall treble stitches grouped together to make a cluster, or separated to create an array. By combining different stitches, you'll be able to make lacy swirls, 'V' shapes and stars, flowers and scallops, each adding more decoration and depth to your crochet.

You need to keep your wits about you and remember where you are in the pattern. A row counter can be useful here and why not keep a pencil and paper nearby to make notes too.

COMBINING STITCHES

READING WRITTEN PATTERNS

As before, each pattern will detail the stitches for each row. These will appear more complicated at first glance, but luckily a few conventions are used to make following them a little easier; often you'll find a set of stitch instructions within a bracket. These stitches are grouped together for a reason and the pattern will explain why.

Row 3: ch 3, turn, (2tr, ch 1, 2tr) in first st.

1. Here the bracket contains a set of stitches that need to be made in the first stitch; two treble crochets, one chain and two more treble crochets.

Row 4: ch 3, turn, *(2tr, ch 1, 2tr) in first st, sk 2 sts, (2tr, ch 1, 2tr) in next st, sk 2 sts* repeat to end of row

1. Sometimes you'll find a set of stitches that need to be repeated across the row or round. These will usually be contained within asterisks.

Okay. Take a deep breath here and read across the row. There's a set of asterisks with a big chunk of pattern within. You will put the stitches in the brackets into the first stitch, skip two stitches, and then put the stitches in the next brackets in the following stitch, skip two stitches. This repeats across the row.

You will often find with these more complicated patterns, the number of stitches in each row isn't given at the end of the instruction.

This is because you don't need to count stitches, but rather ensure that the correct number of stitch sequences is followed. If you make it to the end of the row with no spare stitches, you've done it!

Admittedly, these written instructions can look a little daunting. There is, after all, a lot of description needed. The best thing to do is to work steadily along the instructions bit by bit, rather than trying to remember the whole line. Well-written instructions will tell you exactly where to put your hook and what to do with it. And once you actually start working through, it all becomes a lot easier, I promise.

Thankfully, many complicated patterns will have a diagram to give you a visual reference. The added bonus is that the stitches and shapes are easy to see and can be simpler to follow than the written pattern. These diagrams will often show a shortened section, particularly if there are pattern repeats. You'll see examples of these as you work through the projects.

SUPER SCARF

What makes this scarf super is the fact that it's humongous and cosy and comfy, but it's not at all bulky. It will keep you warm without feeling like a weight around your neck. This is because it's crocheted using a huge 15mm (US Q) hook in mesh stitch, which creates an airy, open texture. Mesh stitch? It's just a treble crochet stitch followed by a chain stitch.

Oh, and it has pom-poms. Everyone loves pom-poms, right?

YOU WILL NEED

I have used...
- 3 x 100g ball Rowan Big Wool in Blue Velvet (shade 026)

You could use...
- Any super-chunky weight yarn and hook to match. A higher wool content will keep you warmer

You will also need...
- 15mm (approx. US Q) hook
- Tapestry needle
- 65mm (2⅜in) Pom-pom maker or make your own (see Embellishments)

Finished size:
23 x 230cm (9 x 90in)

CHART

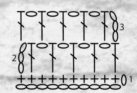

MAKING UP

Tie your pom-poms to each corner and weave in ends. Now wear your scarf long, Bohemian style or wrapped around as many times as it'll fit. You'll be super warm in your super scarf, no matter how cold it is outside.

PATTERN

Your first job is to make four pom-poms. Leave each with a 20cm (8in) tail for sewing onto the scarf later.

Foundation chain: ch 16
Row 1: (ch 1) dc 16
Row 2: (ch 3, turn) tr 1 in 5th chain from hook, *ch 1, sk st, tr 1* repeat across
Row 3: (ch 3, turn) *tr 1 in ch-1 space, ch 1* repeat across. Tr 1 in top of ch-3 from previous row

Rows 4–72: (approx.) repeat row 3
Row 73: (ch 1, turn) dc 16 Fasten off (see Fastening off) and weave in ends (see Weaving in ends).

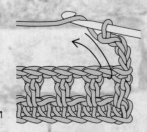

OTHER THINGS TO TRY

You could easily make this scarf wider – just increase the number of stitches across the row. Make sure you have an even number of stitches in your foundation chain and this pattern will work perfectly. Or how about making an infinity or loop scarf? Just leave off the pom-poms and sew the shorter edges together.

Adding new yarn to your work

This scarf uses every last scrap of your three balls of yarn, so you'll need to know how to add new yarn to your work. When you reach the end of your old yarn you need to leave a 15cm (5in) tail. Work a treble crochet stitch as usual until you are left with two loops on the hook. Hold the old yarn tail out of the way and the new yarn tail in your right hand. Yarn over with the new yarn and pull through the loops to complete the stitch. Work a few more stitches before tying the ends together (you will weave them out of sight at the end).

SLOUCHY ANKLE WARMERS

You've packed away your winter boots, the spring sunshine is beckoning, but my goodness, it's still a bit chilly in the mornings. Keep your legs toasty-warm with these sweet little ankle warmers. Crocheted in soft and cosy yarn, they combine alternate rows of 'V' stitch with groups of treble crochet to create a pretty, yet simple pattern.

YOU WILL NEED

I have used...
• 1 x 100g ball Rowan Creative Focus Worsted in Mulch (shade 06)

You could use...
• Any Aran or Worsted weight yarn with hook to match

You will also need...
• 7mm (US approx. K/L) hook
• Tapestry needle

Finished size:
29 x 27cm (11½ x 10½in)

CHART

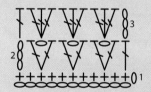

PATTERN

(Make 2)

Foundation chain: ch 44
Row 1: (ch 1) dc 44
Row 2: (ch 3, turn) (tr 1, ch 1, tr 1) in 6th st from hook *sk 2 sts (tr 1, ch 1, tr 1) in next st* repeat along the row until you have 2 sts left, then sk st, tr 1 in last st.
Row 3: (ch 3, turn) 3tr in each ch-1 space along the row. For final stitch, tr 1 in top of ch-3 from row below.

Rows 4 to 21: Repeat Rows 2 and 3 alternately. Leave a 70cm (27½in) tail for making up.

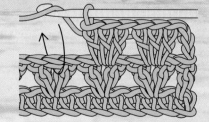

MAKING UP

With right side (RS) facing you (the tail from the foundation chain will be at the bottom left corner), turn the outside edges into the middle and thread the tapestry needle with the long tail. Stitch the two sides together, making sure that there are no big gaps along the seams. Then fasten off (see Fastening off), weave in ends (see Weaving in ends) and turn out the right way. These little ankle warmers are perfect to warm that gap between your skinny jeans and your summer pumps. No more cold ankles for you.

Adjusting the pattern

It's easy to adjust this pattern: If you want longer or shorter ankle warmers then simply add or subtract rows. If you need to alter the width, simply change the length of the foundation chain – just ensure the total number of stitches is a multiple of three, then add two more.

OTHER THINGS TO TRY

Why not make this pattern double the width? You'd have a rather lovely cowl and if you made this pattern much narrower, you could make a cute pair of wrist warmers, too!

51

WHIMSICAL COLLAR

The perfect addition to an otherwise boring outfit, an adorable crochet collar will add a touch of class and is a speedy easy project to boot. You'll still be working in rows, but this time each one is different, creating pretty detailing and a fancy scalloped edge

YOU WILL NEED

I have used...
- 1 x 50g ball of Rowan Handknit Cotton in: Linen (shade 205)

You could use...
- Any DK yarn and hook to match.

You will also need...
- 4mm hook (US 6/G) hook
- 1m x 2.5mm (39 ⅜ x ⅛in) suede/leather cord or ribbon
- Wooden beads
- Tapestry needle

Finished size:
39.5 x 4cm (15¼ x 4in)

CHART

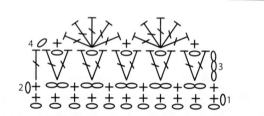

MAKING UP

Thread cord or ribbon through the second row of your collar, thread the beads onto the ends and tie a knot to secure them. Decisions, decisions... should you wear the collar with the natty bow to the front or the back? It's up to you. Just make sure it's accompanied by a jaunty smile and add a little whimsy to your wardrobe.

PATTERN

Foundation chain: ch 71
Row 1: (ch 1) dc 71
Row 2: (ch 1, turn) dc 1, *ch 2, sk 1, dc 1* repeat across row
Row 3: (ch 3, turn) (tr 1, ch 1, tr 1) in each ch-2 sp along. Tr 1 in the final st.

Row 4: (ch 1, turn) dc 1 in 1st ch-1 sp, *5tr in next ch-1 sp, dc 1 in following ch-1 sp* repeat across row.
Fasten off (see Fastening off) and weave in ends (see Weaving in ends).

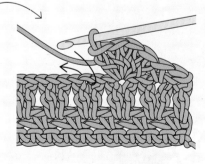

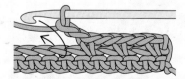

Adjusting the pattern

If you want to make a longer or shorter collar simply increase or decrease the number of chains in the foundation row. Make sure your total number of chains is a multiple of four and add three more and the pattern will work perfectly.

OTHER THINGS TO TRY

Although cotton yarns work really
well with this pattern, you can always
experiment. It might be fun to
choose a fluffy mohair yarn to make
a winter collar, or even some super-
chunky yarn for a mega version.

MAKING THE ROUNDS

So far in this book you have worked in rows, back and forth, back and forth, turning and turning your work. Not anymore! Say hello to working in one direction – round and round. It's no more difficult than crocheting in rows and, once you've mastered the basics, it'll open up a whole new world of creative possibilities.

I've already mentioned that there are two different ways of working with circles: flat (think rugs, coasters, tablemats) and 3-dimensional (hats, bags, and toys). For both of these, you begin your crochet not with a row, but a circle and you work around, increasing and decreasing stitches to create shaping and height.

Sometimes when you crochet in a circle, you will join the end of one round to the beginning of the next. This is called a 'joined round'. You'll need to do this when making a motif like a doily, or a granny square. At the beginning of each round, you make a chain of stitches to mimic the height of the stitch, but unlike a turning chain, you don't turn.

Other times, you crochet in continuous rounds. Here, there's no joining and no chains. You just keep going on and on and on and on. You'll do this mostly when the pattern calls for just one stitch throughout, (often double crochet) and is usually when making toys, or something requiring a dense stitch, such as a hat.

Right, let's get on with making some circles...

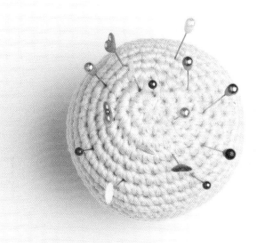

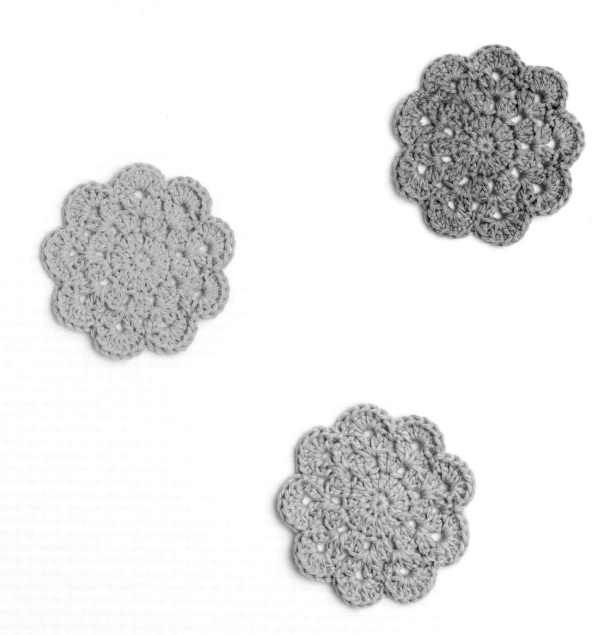

MAKING CIRCLES

There are three methods for starting off in the round and a pattern should advise you. Each one works equally well, so try them all and see which one you prefer. Make sure you have a stitch marker at the ready. We'll start with double crochet, but these methods also work for the taller stitches.

CHAIN 2 METHOD

So-called because you begin with a chain of two stitches.

Round 1: ch 2, 6dc in 2nd chain from hook

1. In the second stitch from the hook, make six double crochet stitches.

2. Count those 'V's. Can you see the six stitches? That's your first round made. After making the next round you can pull the yarn tail to tighten the hole slightly.

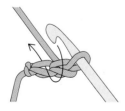

Don't worry about overcrowding — your stitch will expand enough to fit these little fellas in.

JOINED CHAIN METHOD

Sometimes, when you need to get more stitches into your first round, you'll want a slightly bigger circle and this can be achieved by making a ring of chain stitches.

Round 1: ch 4 and join with a sl st. 9dc in ring.

1. First, make a chain of four stitches. Next you need to know how to make a joining stitch and there is a jolly useful little stitch called a slip stitch (sl st), which is perfect for this task. A slip stitch has no height at all and so does not interfere with the stitches you have made.

2. Insert your hook into the first chain stitch.

3. Yarn over hook and pull through all the loops on your hook.

4. Make one chain (which doesn't count as a stitch here) and then put nine double crochets into the centre hole of the ring itself, not the stitches. Put your hook through the ring, yarn over and make a double crochet in the usual way. Make the other eight double crochet stitches.

MAGIC CIRCLE METHOD

This method creates a circle, which can be tightened so that the hole in the middle can be made almost invisible. In a pattern it might be written as:

Round 1: 6dc in magic ring

1. Make a loop with the yarn so that the tail end is behind the working yarn.

2. Hold the point where it crosses with your thumb and finger.

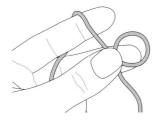

3. Insert your hook through the circle and pull the yarn through.

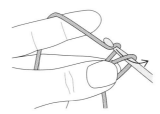

4. Yarn over and pull the yarn through again. This anchors the yarn.

5. Now make six double crochets into the circle, working over the two strands of yarn.

6. Pull slowly and firmly on the yarn tail and watch the circle close tightly.

CROCHETING IN CONTINUOUS ROUNDS

Round 2: 2dc in each st (12 sts)

1. With six double crochets in your beginning circle you need to make two double crochets in each stitch around. Make your first double crochet and insert your stitch marker. Then make another double crochet in the same stitch. Continue around, putting two double crochets in each stitch. You will have 12 stitches at the end of this round.

Round 3: *dc 1, 2dc in next stitch* repeat around (18 sts)

1. In this round, the increases are less frequent. Remove your stitch marker and make one double crochet in the first stitch. Re-insert the stitch marker. Now make two double crochets in the following stitch. Repeat this around: One double crochet in the first stitch, two double crochets in the next. You will have 18 stitches.

With this method of circle-making, it's really important that you use a stitch marker to show where the beginning of each round is, as it all looks the same. But what to do if it falls out when you're working? Just reinsert it roughly where you think it came from. It really won't affect your pattern enough to worry about.

CROCHETING IN JOINED ROUNDS

Anything that uses a decorative stitch will be worked in this way.

Round 1: ch 2, 6dc in 2nd stitch from hook or 6dc in magic circle. Sl st to top of ch-2 to join round

1. For the practise, begin a chain of two, then make six double crochets in your beginning circle. Join the round by making a slip stitch (see Joined chain method and Making a slip stitch) into the top of the chain-two.

Round 2: ch 3 (counts as first tr), tr 1 in the same st, 2tr in each st around. Sl st into top of ch-3 to join round (12 sts)

1. Here, you make a chain of three (which is pretending to be a treble stitch). Put your stitch marker in the third chain and then make another treble crochet in the same stitch (look to see where you joined the round with the slip stitch – this is where you put the treble stitch).

2. Now make two treble stitches in every stitch around. You will have 11 treble stitches in total and one chain-of-three-masquerading-as-a-treble with your stitch marker in the top.

3. Next, to join the round. Simply make a slip stitch into the top of the chain-three (marked by the stitch marker).

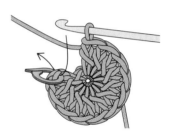

THE INVISIBLE DECREASE

This is an easy variation of the dc2tog stitch. It gives an almost invisible finish to your decreases when you work in the round. You can use the invisible decrease method whenever you see 'dc2tog' in a pattern.

1. To make the stitch, insert your hook under the front loop of the first stitch, then under the front loop of the second stitch (you will have three loops on your hook).

2. Yarn over hook and pull the yarn through the first two loops.

3. Yarn over and pull through both loops. You'll barely be able to see your decreases.

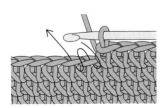

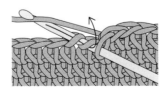

Have a practise of these techniques if you like, or if you're ready why not try the projects? They'll give you the opportunity to try out your new skills and will get you going round and round in circles!

COASTAL COASTERS

Crocheted in muted beachy hues, these cotton coasters are the perfect companion to your morning coffee. Apart from looking stylish, they will keep those nasty drips from spoiling your table and are completely washable and hardwearing. What's not to love?

YOU WILL NEED

I have used...

- 1 x 50g ball Sirdar Simply Recycled DK in: Clay (shade 13), Denim (shade 16), Fleck (shade 18) and Pollen (shade 19)

You could use...

- Any yarn and hook to match, just remember that the heavier the weight, the bigger the coaster

You will also need...

- 4mm (US 6/G) hook
- Stitch marker
- Tapestry needle

Finished size:

9cm (3½in)

PATTERN

Round 1: ch 4 and join with a sl st. 9dc in ring or 9dc in magic circle. Sl st into 1st dc to join round

Round 2: ch 3 (counts as first tr) and tr 1 in the same st, 2tr in each st around. Sl st into top of ch-3 to join round (18 sts)

Round 3: ch 3 (counts as first tr) and 2tr in the same st. *sk st, 3tr in next st* repeat around. Sl st into top of ch-3 to join round (27 sts)

Round 4: sl st across to first space between 3tr group. (ch 3 (counts as tr), tr 1, ch 2, 2tr in the same space), *(2tr, ch 2, 2tr) in next space*. Repeat around. Sl st to top of ch-3 to join round.

Round 5: sl st across to first ch-2 space. (ch 3 (counts as tr) 6tr in ch-2 sp), dc 1 in space between group, *7tr in ch-2 sp, dc 1 in space between group* repeat around. Sl st to top of ch-3 to join round. Fasten off (see Fastening off) and weave in ends (see Weaving in ends).

CHART

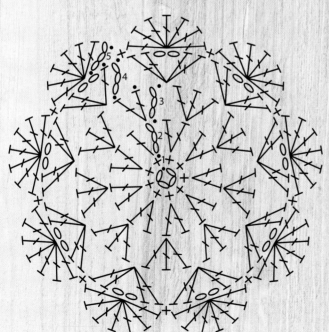

MAKING UP

Arrange decoratively on your coffee table, add a beverage of your fancy and admire.

Troubleshooting

These coasters will need washing to remove the remains of your coffee and you might find they're a little crumpled afterwards. Gently press with an iron on the reverse of the coaster. Don't be too heavy-handed though or you'll spoil the stitches.

HANDY PINCUSHION

A pincushion is a very useful thing. A jar to store your crafting pretties is another very useful thing. A pincushion and jar combo? Surely a match made in craft-room heaven!

Created entirely in double crochet, this simple little project uses continuous rounds to form a sphere, and you'll use the increases and decreases you already know to shape the pincushion.

YOU WILL NEED

I have used...
- 1 x 50g ball Drops Paris Cotton Aran in Off White (shade 17)

You could use...
- Any yarn and hook to match. This project uses a tiny amount of yarn, so is perfect for any leftovers from previous projects

You will also need...
- 4.5mm (US 7) hook
- Tapestry needle
- Toy stuffing
- Jam jar (the lid of mine measures 6cm (2½in) diameter, but any should work)
- Ribbon wide enough to cover the side of the lid
- PVA or similar glue

Finished size:
10 x 7cm (4 x 2¾in)

PATTERN

Round 1: ch 2, 6dc in 2nd st from hook or 6dc in magic ring
Round 2: 2dc in each st around (12 sts)
Round 3: 2dc in each st around (24 sts)
Rounds 4–5: dc 24
Round 6: *dc 1, 2dc in next stitch*. Repeat around (36 sts)
Round 7: *dc 5, 2dc in next stitch*. Repeat around (42 sts)
Rounds 8–13: dc 42

Round 14: *dc 5, dc2tog*. Repeat around (36 sts)
Use the invisible decrease method here (see The invisible decrease) if you like.

Round 15: *dc 4, dc2tog*. Repeat around (30 sts)
Round 16: dc 30
Round 17: dc2tog around (15 sts)
Fasten off (see Fastening off) and weave in ends (see Weaving in ends).

Right side, wrong side

This is a good place to talk about the right and wrong side of your work, because when you work in one direction, your crochet has a very different front and back.

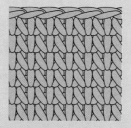 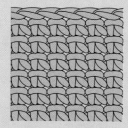

The right side is the one with continuous 'V' stitches.

The wrong side has a row of 'V's and a row of dashes.

When I crochet, the right side usually ends up on the inside. If you find the same then simply turn your work out the right way.

MAKING UP

Stuff firmly. Then stick the pincushion to the lid of the jam jar and the ribbon around the edge of the lid with glue. Allow to dry and then use to store all your wonderful goodies!

OTHER THINGS TO TRY

You could make the pincushion taller. All you need to do is repeat rows 8–13 as many times as desired. Or why not make a whole set of these using different sized jam jars. You'll never lose anything again!

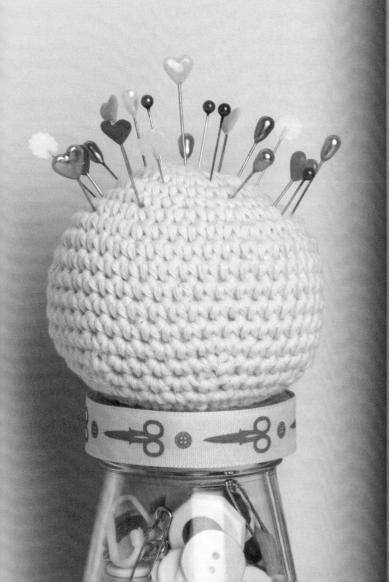

BERTIE AND BETTY BEAR

This style of crochet is called 'amigurumi', which is Japanese for 'crocheted or knitted toy'. Amigurumi patterns are crocheted in continuous rounds of double crochet and, despite looking tricky, are easy to make. Bertie and Betty are exactly the same pattern. I had to make two because Bertie seemed lonely on his own.

YOU WILL NEED:

I have used...
- For Bertie: 1 x 50g ball Rico Creative Cotton Aran in Clay (shade 51)
- For Betty: 1 x 50g ball Rico Creative Cotton Aran in Light Blue (shade 32)

You could use...
- These bears can be made with practically any yarn you like. Anything from DK to Aran works well.

You will also need...
- 4.5mm (US 7) hook
- 2 x 6mm (¼in) Safety eyes
- Felt or fabric for nose and tummy patch
- Embroidery thread in brown for nose and complimentary colour for sewing the tummy patch
- Embroidery needle
- Tapestry needle
- Toy stuffing
- PVA or similar glue
- Small length of 6mm (¼in) wide ribbon for bow

Finished size:
10 x 7cm (4 x 2¾in)

PATTERN

Head and body

(Make 1)

Round 1: ch 2, 5dc in 2nd st from hook or 5dc in magic ring
Round 2: 2dc in each st around (10 sts)
Round 3: 2dc in each st around (20 sts)
Round 4: dc 20
Round 5: *dc 1, 2dc in next st.* Repeat around (30 sts)
Rounds 6–11: dc 30
Round 12: *dc 1, dc2tog*. Repeat around (20 sts)
Round 13: dc 20

Here, you need to add the safety eyes. Insert them between rows 10 and 11, roughly six stitches apart. Begin stuffing the head.

Round 14: dc2tog around (10 sts)

Finish stuffing the head. It needs to be quite firm.

Round 15: dc 10
Round 16: *dc 1, 2dc in next st*. Repeat around (15 sts)
Round 17: dc 15
Round 18: *dc 2, 2dc in next st*. Repeat around (20 sts)
Round 19: dc 20
Round 20: *dc 3, 2dc in next st*. Repeat around (25 sts)
Rounds 21–24: dc 25
Round 25: *dc 4, 2dc in next st*. Repeat around (30 sts)
Rounds 26–27: dc 30
Round 28: *dc 1, dc2tog*. Repeat around (20 sts)
Round 29: dc 20

Begin stuffing the body.

Round 30: dc2tog around (10 sts)

Finish stuffing the body.

Round 31: dc2tog x 3, leaving the remaining stitches unworked (7 sts) Sew closed (see Making up) and weave in ends. (see Weaving in ends).

Arms

(Make 2)

Round 1: ch 2, 4dc in 2nd st from hook or 4dc in magic ring
Round 2: 2dc in each st around (8 sts)
Rounds 3–5: dc 8
Round 6: *dc 2, dc2tog*. Repeat once (6 sts)

Stuff the hand firmly. You don't need to stuff the arms.

Rounds 7–13: dc 6
Fasten off (see Fastening off) and leave a 30cm (12in) tail for sewing to the body later.

Legs

(Make 2)

Round 1: ch 2, 5dc in 2nd st from hook or 5dc in magic ring
Round 2: 2dc in each st around (10 sts)
Rounds 3–5: dc 10

Begin stuffing.

Round 6: *dc 3, dc2tog*. Repeat once (8 sts)
Rounds 7–9: dc 8
Round 10: dc2tog, dc 6 (7 sts)
Rounds 11–13: dc 7
Finish stuffing firmly. Fasten off and leave a 30cm (12in) tail for sewing to the body later.

Ears

(Make 2)

Round 1: ch 2, 6dc in 2nd st from hook or 6dc in magic ring
Round 2: 2dc in each st around (12 sts)
Round 3: *dc 1, 2dc in next st*. Repeat around (18 sts)
Round 4: dc 18
Round 5: dc2tog around (9 sts)

Sew closed and leave a 30cm (12in) tail for sewing to the head.

MAKING UP

Sewing the body and ears closed and hiding ends

Thread the tapestry needle with the long-tail end and weave it under the back loops of the stitches of the final round. Gently pull and like magic the hole is closed. Now secure the thread by making a little knot (weave the needle under a stitch and then through the loop you've just made). All that's left to do is hide that yarn-tail, so poke your needle into the bear and out through the other side. Pull the yarn taut, and carefully snip it away, as close to the bear as you dare! The end will retract slightly and disappear back inside the body part.

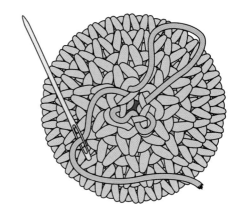

Sewing the parts to the bear

There's no magic trick to sewing the limbs in place, it just takes a little patience.

1. Thread the tapestry needle with the long yarn tail.

2. Decide where you want the part placed.

3. Hold the part in place and sew small stitches between those on the limb and those on the body to secure it. The key is to work methodically around the limb, ensuring there are no gaps. You only need a few stitches to do this.

4. Don't fasten off or hide any yarn tails until you're happy with your placement.

5. Once you are happy, then snip away!

OTHER THINGS TO TRY

You can easily alter the shape of these bears. How about making the body shorter, or making longer legs and arms? All you need to do is increase or decrease the number of rows you make.

Final touches

Cut a little circle from the felt (I drew around a button) and use brown embroidery thread to stitch a nose. Use the glue to stick the nose to the face, or you can stitch it if you prefer. Then cut an oval tummy patch (it doesn't have to be a perfect shape) and using embroidery thread in whatever colour you like, use an overstitch to attach the patch to the body (see Sewing trim). Tie the ribbon around the bear's neck.

And that is how to crochet a bear. It's really bear-y simple.

GREAT
GRANNIES

Probably one of the strangest names for a crochet technique, grannies are so-called because in the days of yore, it used to be our Nannas and Grandmas who worked tirelessly in the evenings to create cosy blankets and shawls to keep us all warm. A granny square is the traditional shape for this style of crochet, made from repeating patterns of three treble crochet stitches and using chain stitches to create corners. Nowadays, grannies can refer to anything that uses this same grouping of treble stitches and can be worked in rows, too.

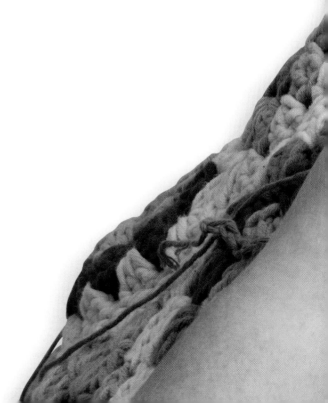

STITCH TUTORIAL:
THE GRANNY SQUARE

Probably the most famous of all crocheted items, granny squares have been used in blanket making for generations. They were particularly popular in the 1970s and were often fashioned into grotesque, itchy tank tops in orange and brown polyester. Thankfully, modern yarn and colour choices have revolutionized the granny square, and crochet designers are turning this old classic into something altogether, well... nicer.

The key to the success of the granny square is its simplicity; the square is worked in joined rounds, each containing groups of treble crochet stitches, separated by chain stitches.

CHART

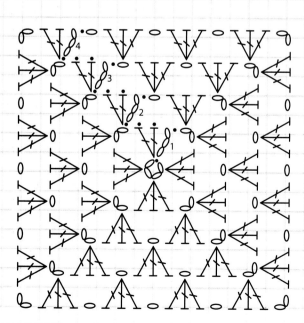

It's easy to spot the progression of a pattern around the square; groups of three treble crochet stitches are interspersed with one chain stitch along the edges and two chain stitches make up the corners.

MAKING A GRANNY SQUARE

Grannies are worked in the round, so you'll need to begin with a circle. This means that the front of your work is the side facing you. You can use any of the methods demonstrated previously (see Making circles). I prefer the magic circle method, but for this practise, let's keep it simple and use a joined chain (see Joined chain method and Making a slip stitch).

Beginning circle: ch 4 and join with a sl st. (creating a ring)

Round 1: ch 3 (counts as tr), working into the ring, 2tr, ch 2, *3tr, ch 2* repeat x 3. Sl st into top of ch-3 to join round.

1. Make a chain of three, then make two treble crochets into the centre of the ring, to make your first group.

2. Chain two stitches, then make three treble crochets into the ring. Repeat this twice more and join the round into the top of the third chain with a slip stitch.

3. You will have four groups of three treble crochets, each separated by a chain of two stitches. (These chains are going to be the corners of your granny square.)

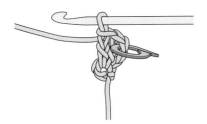

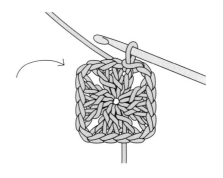

Round 2: sl st across to 1st ch-2 space. (Ch 3 (counts as tr), 2tr, ch 2, 3tr) in same ch-2 space, ch 1, *(3tr, ch 2, 3tr) in next ch-2 space, ch 1* repeat x 3. Sl st into top of ch-3 to join round.

1. Slip stitch across the first two treble crochets and into the first chain-two space. This is where you will put your first corner group, so make a chain of three and two treble crochets, followed by a chain of two (the corner) and another three treble crochets.

2. Chain one and then make the corner group in the next chain-two space – three treble crochets, two chain stitches, three treble crochets. Repeat this into all the corners and join the round into the top of the third chain with a slip stitch.

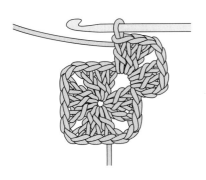

At the beginning of each round you need to chain one and then make the first double crochet stitch in the same stitch. At the end of the round, you make the joining slip stitch into the top of the first double crochet stitch, ignoring the chain stitch and continue as before.

Round 3: sl st across to 1st ch-2 space. (Ch 3 (counts as tr), 2tr, ch 2, 3tr) in 1st ch-2 space, ch 1, *3tr in next ch-1 space, ch 1, (3tr, ch 2, 3tr) in next ch-2 space, ch 1* repeat x 3. Sl st into top of ch-3 to join round.

1. This round begins in exactly the same way, by making the corner group (three treble crochets, two chain stitches, three treble crochets).

2. Next, you need to chain one and make three treble crochets in the chain-one space.

3. Chain one and make another corner group. Repeat the pattern around the square until you reach the beginning and join with a slip stitch as before.

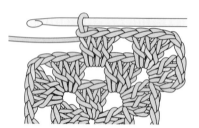

Round 4: sl st across to 1st ch-2 space. (Ch 3 (counts as tr), 2tr, ch 2, 3tr) in 1st ch-2 space, ch 1, *3tr in next ch-1 space, ch 1, 3 tr in next ch-1 space, ch 1, (3tr, ch 2, 3tr) in next ch-2 space, ch 1* repeat x 3. Sl st into top of ch-3 to join round.

1. As before, make the corner group (three treble crochets, two chain stitches, three treble crochets).

2. Next, you need to chain one and make three treble crochets in the chain-one space. Repeat this again as you've got another chain-one space coming next.

3. Chain one and make another corner group. Repeat around the square until you reach the beginning and join with a slip stitch as before.

BEYOND ROUND 4:

You are probably beginning to get a feel for this pattern by now: in each chain-two space put a corner group (three treble crochets, two chain stitches, three treble crochets), and in each chain-one space put a single treble group (three treble crochets). Each of these groups is separated by one chain stitch.

CHANGING COLOUR AND WORKING OVER ENDS

1. After you have finished a round, slip stitch into the chain-two space in the corner so you're ready for the new round. Cut the yarn, leaving a 10cm (4in) tail and pull it through the final stitch, fastening off (see Fastening off).

2. Now knot this end together with your new colour, at the back of your work, as close to the stitches as you can.

3. Put your hook through the chain-two space, yarn over in the new colour and pull the yarn through the space.

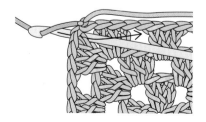

4. Yarn over and make three chain stitches as usual.

5. Repeat this whenever you want to change colour at the beginning of a round.

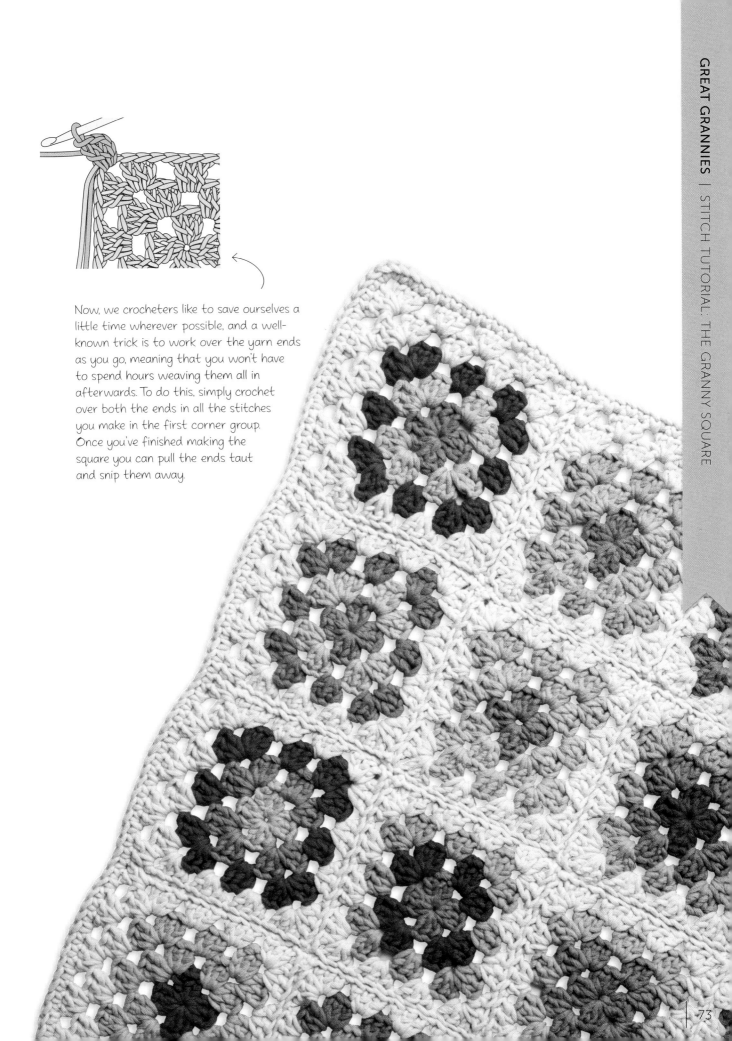

Now, we crocheters like to save ourselves a little time wherever possible, and a well-known trick is to work over the yarn ends as you go, meaning that you won't have to spend hours weaving them all in afterwards. To do this, simply crochet over both the ends in all the stitches you make in the first corner group. Once you've finished making the square you can pull the ends taut and snip them away.

HEIRLOOM BLANKET

I love handmade blankets. They are lovely to cosy up with on chilly evenings, or snuggle under on movie night. Plus they make a wonderful present for a new baby, a new house or even a new puppy. I have used seven different colours. Six of the yarns were used in a random order to create the first three rounds of each square. The final, fourth round of each was completed in the cream (Pebble) colour. This colour was also used to join each square and provide the edging.

YOU WILL NEED

I have used...

- 7 x 100g ball Rowan All Seasons Chunky in Pebble (shade 601)
- 2 x 100g ball Rowan All Seasons Chunky in: Drift (shade 603) and Shore (shade 604)
- 1 x 100g ball Rowan All Seasons Chunky in: Jetsam (shade 609), Stoney (shade 610), Samphire (shade 611), Flotsam (shade 612)

You could use...

- Any yarn and hook to match. Chunkier yarn makes bigger grannies, so you'll need fewer of them to make a blanket (not that I'm lazy, or anything...).

You will also need...

- 7mm (US 10.5-11/ K-L) hook
- Tapestry needle

Finished size:

1 x 1m (39½ x 39½in)

PATTERN

(Make 49)

Beginning circle: ch 4 with your chosen first colour and join with a sl st or use the magic ring method (see Magic ring method)

Round 1: ch 3 (counts as tr) 2tr, ch 2, *3tr, ch 2* repeat x 3. Sl st into top of ch-3 to join round, sl st across to 1st ch-2 space.

Round 2: change colour, (ch 3 (counts as tr), 2tr, ch 2, 3tr) in 1st ch-2 space, ch 1, *(3tr, ch 2, 3tr) in next ch-2 space, ch 1* repeat x 3. Sl st into top of ch-3 to join round, sl st across to 1st ch-2 space.

Round 3: change colour, (ch 3 (counts as tr), 2tr, ch 2, 3tr) in 1st ch-2 space, ch 1, *3tr in next ch-1 space, ch 1, (3tr, ch 2, 3tr) in next ch-2 space, ch 1* repeat x 3. Sl st into top of ch-3 to join round, sl st across to 1st ch-2 space.

Round 4: change colour, (ch 3 (counts as tr), 2tr, ch 2, 3tr) in 1st ch-2 space, ch 1, *3tr in next ch-1 space, ch 1, 3tr in next ch-1 space, ch 1, (3tr, ch 2, 3tr) in next ch-2 space, ch 1* repeat x 3. Sl st into top of ch-3 to join round. Fasten off (see Fastening off).

MAKING UP

Stitching the squares together

There are lots of different ways to join granny squares; for this project we are using 'whip stitch'. Whip-stitching is a great method for joining seams, as it is quick and produces a secure finish. Remember to use the same coloured yarn as the final round of the square, so your stitching won't show.

1. Decide on the arrangement of squares – you may like to lay them out first, or pick them randomly.

2. Decide on your first row of seven squares. (You will join these to make a row.)

3. Take two squares and hold them with right sides (RS) together. Look at how the stitches match up – you'll be sewing these together through the back loops (the loops furthest away from each other).

4. Thread a tapestry needle with a 50cm (19½in) of your chosen yarn colour and begin in the corner of the squares, making a stitch through the back loops only. Sew over this stitch again to secure the yarn, leaving a tail of 13cm (5in) for sewing in later.

5. Insert the needle through the next pair of stitches (back loops) and pull the yarn through. Don't over-tighten it or your squares will look a bit wonky.

6. Bring your needle back through the next pair of stitches. Continue along the edge of the square, sewing through the back loops of all the pairs.

7. Once you've reached the final corner, fasten off, weave in ends (see Weaving in ends) and cut the tails away.

8. Add another square to the two you have joined. Repeat steps 3–7 until you have a row of seven squares.

9. Repeat steps 2–8 until you have seven rows.

Stitching the rows together

1. Take two rows and hold them with RS together.

2. Cut a length of yarn 150cm (59in) long and sew whip stitches along from one corner, across the entire row. It's worth doubling back over the corner stitches so that you don't end up with holes where the corners join.

3. Repeat this until all the rows are joined together.

4. Fasten off and weave in ends.

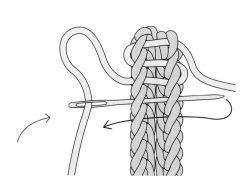

Edging the blanket

The blanket needs some edging to pull the project together and tidy up the sides. You will need to do two rounds. The first is a continuation of the granny square pattern and the second is a round of double crochet, just like we did with the dishcloths (see Simple Dishcloths). If you want to try something a bit more fancy, then have a look at the section on Edging (see Edging).

With RS facing you, attach the yarn onto your hook with a slip knot (see Making a slip knot) and insert your hook in the chain-2 space at the right-hand corner of the blanket.

OTHER THINGS TO TRY

Granny squares can be used for a multitude of projects: cushions and bedspreads, ponchos, scarves and bags. Simply adjust the number of squares to create smaller or larger designs. Remember the corner groups and your shaping will be fine. Add a few rows of edging and you're done!

Round 1: using your chosen colour, (ch 3 (counts as tr), 2tr, ch 2, 3tr) in ch-2 space, ch 1, *(3tr in next ch-1 space, ch 1 repeat x 3) 2tr in next ch-2 space, 2tr in next ch-2 space, ch 1* repeat across the edge, ending with 3tr, ch 2, 3tr in the corner. Repeat around all sides of the blanket. Sl st to top of ch-3 to join round.

Yikes! This round looks a lot more complicated than it is. Make the corner group (chain of three, two treble crochets, chain two, three treble crochets) and then work along the edge, making three treble crochet groups separated by a chain stitch each time. The only difference in the pattern is when you reach the point where the two corners of the grannies are joined (the chain-two spaces). Here, you make two treble stitches in each (no chain stitch needed to separate them) and then carry on your merry way as before.

Round 2: ch 1, dc 2, *3dc in ch-2 space, dc 121 across row* Repeat on each side of the blanket. Sl st to ch 1 to join round. Fasten off and weave in the ends.

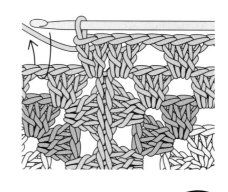

Don't worry about counting the stitches around the edge. As long as you make one double crochet across all the stitches and put three double crochets in each corner, you'll be fine.

THE GRANNY STRIPE

The granny stripe is a version of the granny square and is worked in rows. It uses the same pattern motif of three treble groups separated by a chain stitch, but it has no corners. It is equally versatile and can be used to make a huge variety of projects. This pattern is very useful when you need to work to a set measurement as it can be made as long or short as needed.

CHART

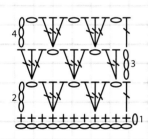

Well, this all looks a little familiar, doesn't it? There's those groups of three treble crochet stitches, separated by a chain stitch again. This time, the pattern doesn't turn any corners; it just keeps going and going and going in rows.

Foundations chain: ch 15

Row 1: (ch 1) dc 15

Row 2: ch 4, turn (counts as tr and ch 1), 3tr in 8th stitch from hook, *ch 1, sk 3 sts, 3tr in next st* repeat across. When there are three stitches left, ch 1, sk 2 sts and tr 1 in the final st.

1. For this row, make a chain of four, turn and then put three treble crochets in the eighth stitch from your hook.

2. Chain one, skip three stitches and put three treble crochets in the next stitch.

3. This pattern repeats across until you have only three stitches left. Don't worry, you haven't made a mistake, you just need to chain one and put one treble crochet in the very last stitch.

Row 3: ch 3, turn (counts as tr), 2tr in ch-1 space, *ch 1, 3tr in ch-1 space* repeat across.

1. Make the treble crochet groups in each chain-one space and make a single chain stitch between them.

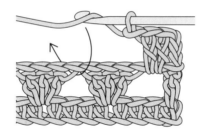

Row 4: ch 4, turn (counts as tr and ch 1), 3tr in 1st ch-1 space, *ch 1, 3tr in next ch-1 space* repeat across. At the end of the row, ch 1 and tr 1 in the final st.

1. For this row, chain four again and make your first group of three treble crochets into the first chain-one space. Chain one and make the next treble crochet groups in the following chain-one space. Repeat along the row. When you've run out of chain-one spaces, chain one and put one treble crochet in the final stitch.

Rows 5 onwards: repeat rows 3 and 4 alternately.

If you're ready for the next project, then let's crack on! It's more granny striping, but with a twist...

GRANNY LAMPSHADE

A lampshade is a funny thing. It sits there unassuming, gathering dust, gradually yellowing with age and one day, you suddenly realize how awful it looks. That's exactly what happened to me. But instead of throwing the offending lampshade in the bin, I decided it could be cured with a bit of crochet. And so the Granny Lampshade was created.

YOU WILL NEED

I have used...

• 1 x 100g ball Sylecraft Special DK in:

A) White (shade 1001)

B) Fondant (shade 1241)

C) Pomegranate (shade 1083)

D) Turquoise (shade 1068

E) Silver (shade 1203)

F) Aspen (1422)

• Bobble trim to fit shade

You could use...

• Any DK to Aran yarn and hook to match

You will also need...

• A lampshade

• 4mm (US 6/G) hook

• Tapestry needle

Finished size:

68.5 x 20cm (27 x 7¾in)

PATTERN

Foundation chain: using colour A, ch 132. Sl st into first chain to join round (make sure your chain isn't twisted)

Round 1: ch 1 (counts as dc), dc 131. Sl st to top of ch-1 to join round. Fasten off yarn (see Fastening off) and attach new colour

Round 2: using colour B, (ch 3 (counts as tr), 2tr) in same st, ch 1, *sk 3 sts, 3tr in next st, ch 1* repeat around. Sl st into top of ch-3 to join round, slip stitch across to the first ch-1 space. Fasten off yarn and attach new colour

Round 3: using colour C, (ch 3 (counts as tr), 2tr) in first ch-1 space, *ch 1, 3tr in next ch-1 space* repeat around. Sl st into top of ch-3 to join round, sl st to first ch-1 space. Fasten off yarn and attach new colour

Rounds 4–24: Repeat round 3

I used the colours in the following order for the remaining rounds:

C, D, E, C, F, A, E, F, D, B, E, D, C, A, F, A, C, E, B, D, F

Fasten off and weave in ends (see Weaving in ends).

OTHER THINGS TO TRY

This project suits any cylindrical object needing a makeover. How about making a pretty pencil holder by jazzing up a plain glass jar with a bit of granny stripe magic?

MAKING UP

Just attach the trim by sewing or gluing and voila!

Adjusting the pattern

Measure around your lampshade. Your foundation chain will need to be roughly the same length, BUT it must be a multiple of four for the pattern to work. Then follow the instructions in the same way. You'll just need to adjust the number of rows to fit the height of your shade.

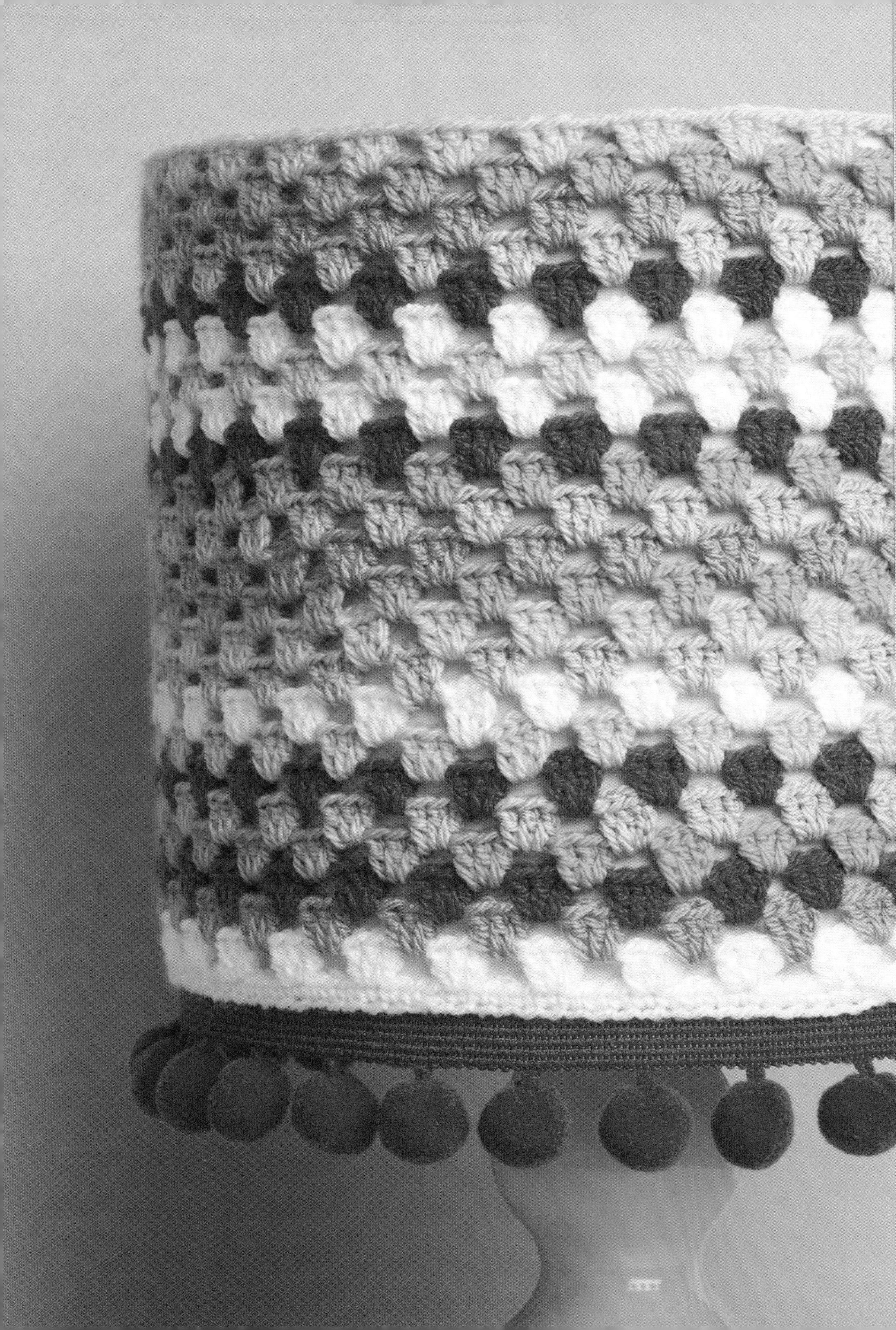

E X T R E M E
CROCHET

A really fun thing about mega-crochet is playing with scale. What happens if you make the Coaster pattern (see Coastal Coasters) with big yarn? Or the Scarf (see Super Scarf)? The mind boggles at the size of Bertie and Betty Bear (see Bertie and Betty Bear) if they were made in T-shirt yarns …

For this type of crochet you need to use the biggest and thickest yarns you can find. Use your imagination, too – you don't have to use commercially manufactured yarn. Think rope, cord, twine, string or make something yourself. There are lots of tutorials online for how to make jumbo yarn from T-shirts, rags, sheets and even plastic bags. A really simple thing to do is to work with lots of strands of yarn at once. Here, you need lots of cheap acrylic DK in whatever colours you like with about 10 strands held together.

Of course, you can purchase ready-made mega yarns for this purpose, too. Choose from a huge variety of super-bulky weight or T-shirt yarn. The three extreme projects in this book use manufactured T-shirt yarn, but any will work as sizing isn't important.

You'll also need a big hook. Anything from 12–20mm (US 17–36) should do the job (your yarn label will advise you, too). But as with all crochet, it's up to you to find what suits the project you are working on.

How to begin? Well, you hold the hook in exactly the same way as you would with a smaller hook and yarn. You'll find it slower to work with initially, but you'll soon get the feel for it and will adjust your grip as you work with it.

There are a few things to bear in mind when using the manufactured T-shirt yarn. First, it stretches. This isn't really a problem, and you'll get used to it, but you'll need to work a little looser to prevent the yarn from becoming too tight. It's also irregular. You may find slubs and nobbles, thin bits, fat bits and strange colours, too. Now, you can either cut these out and re-join the yarn or you can just go with the flow and accept that's how it is. Lastly, the bobbins of yarn are big and heavy, so I find the best way to work is with it by my feet.

YARNY BASKET

Do you find yourself oooo-ing and ahhhh-ing over wool? Ah, yes. Occupational hazard, I'm afraid. You are acquiring what we in the business call a 'stash'. Your stash is important. It will contain new balls in anticipation of future projects and smaller remnants from things previously made. And it needs to be kept away from the spouse/kids/dog and the cat. Especially the cat. And so, dear reader, I have designed a yarny basket to keep your stash safe. This project is crocheted using T-shirt yarn in joined rounds.

YOU WILL NEED

I have used...
- 1 x bobbin Hoooked Zpagetti in:
  A) Grey
  B) Violet

You could use...
- Any extreme yarn and hook to match (buy something different or make your own, whatever you like)

You will also need...
- 15mm (US approx. 15 N/P – Q) hook
- Tapestry needle

Finished size:
36 x 24cm (14 x 9½in)

OTHER THINGS TO TRY

Make more of them! Make the basket taller by increasing the number of rounds or make the basket smaller by stopping the increases at round 6 and continuing with rounds of 35 stitches. You can always leave off the shaping for the handles, too.

PATTERN

At the beginning of each round you need to chain one and then make the first double crochet stitch in the same stitch. At the end of the round, you make the joining slip stitch into the top of the first double crochet stitch, ignoring the chain stitch and continue as before.

Round 1: using colour A, 5dc in magic ring or ch 2, 5dc in 2nd st from hook
Round 2: 2dc in each st around (10 sts)
Round 3: 2dc in each st around (20 sts)
Round 4: *dc 1, 2dc in next st*. Repeat around (30 sts)
Round 5: dc 30
Round 6: *dc 5, 2dc in next st*. Repeat around (35 sts)

Round 7: *dc 1, 2dc in next st*, repeat around, dc 1 in last st (52 sts)
Round 8: dc 52 (BLO)
Rounds 9–16: dc 52
Rounds 17–18: using colour B, dc 52
Round 19: dc 9, ch 8, sk 8 sts, dc 18, ch 8, sk 8 sts, dc 9 (52 sts)
This round shapes the handles for the basket.
Round 20: dc 9, dc 10 in ch-8 space, dc 18, dc 10 in ch-8 space, dc 9 (56 sts)
Round 21: dc 56. Sl st to 1st dc of round to join. Fasten off (see Fastening off) and weave in ends (see Weaving in ends).

MAKING UP

Add your yarn and enjoy the fact that the cat will have a job getting at your stash.

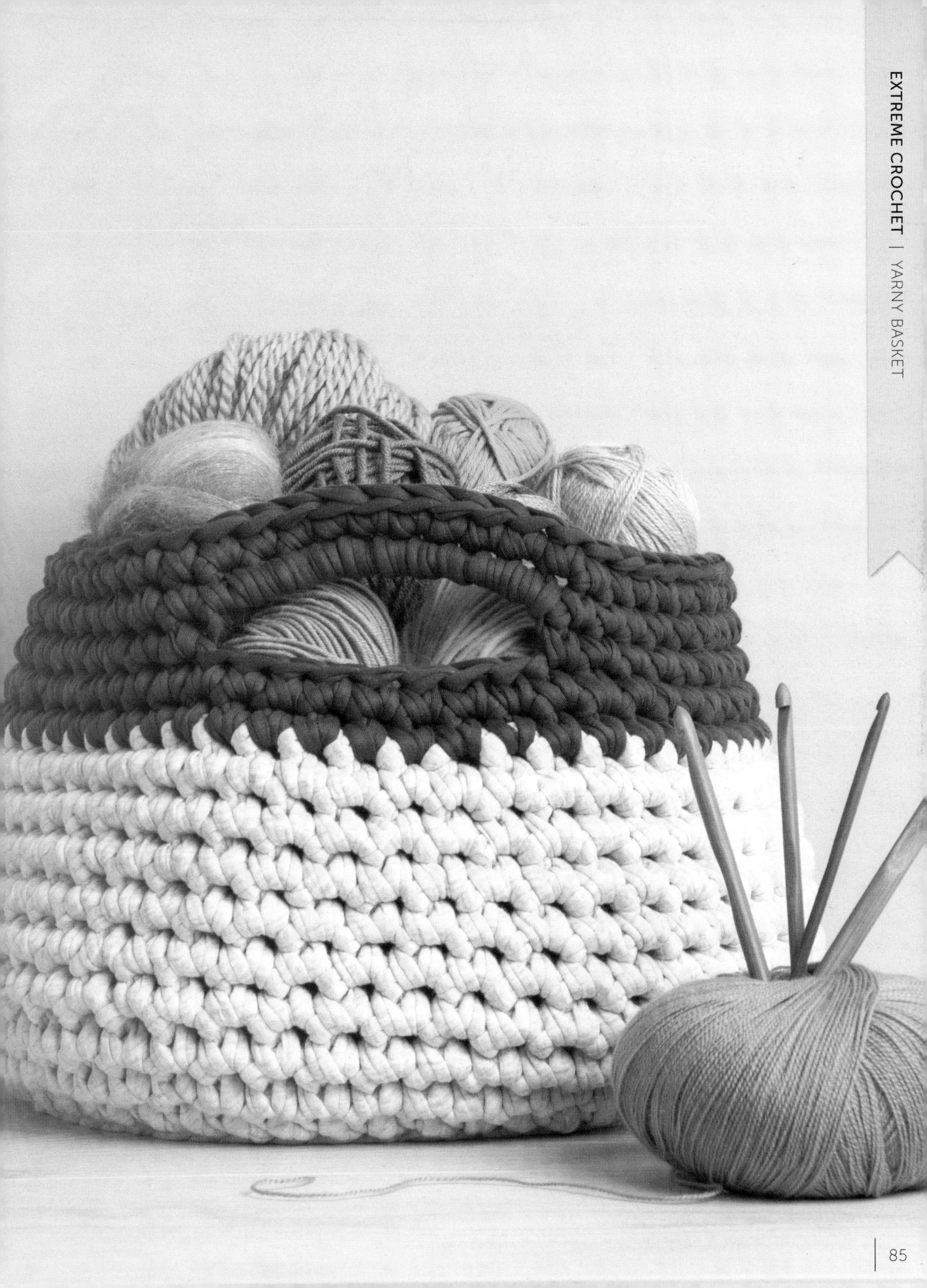

BESIDE THE SEASIDE BATHMAT

This nautical bathmat is crocheted in classic navy and white T-shirt yarn. You'll be crocheting around both sides of the chain to start off working in the round for this project — a new technique that's very easy. I'm going to show you a version of the half-treble crochet stitch that produces an amazing knit-like effect.

YOU WILL NEED

I have used...
- 1 x bobbin Hoooked Zpagetti in:
  A) Marine
  B) White

You could use...
- Any extreme yarn and hook to match

You will also need...
- 15mm (US approx. 15 N/P – Q) hook
- Tapestry needle

Finished size:
65 x 44cm (25½ x 17¼in)

Making the htr knit stitch

This special half-treble crochet stitch produces a knitted effect. As you know, when crocheting, each stitch produces a front loop and a back loop (the 'V'). However, the half-treble stitch produces one more loop, the third loop, right at the back and it is this loop you will work through.

OTHER THINGS TO TRY

This bathmat would work well in any short and stumpy stitch, so plain half-treble crochet or double crochet stitches would be perfect. If you wanted to make your bathmat longer, add stitches to the foundation chain — the increases around the edges will stay the same. If you want a bigger bathmat then keep adding rounds.

PATTERN

The bathmat is worked in joined rounds. At the beginning of each round you need to make a chain of two stitches, and then make the first half-treble stitch in the same stitch. At the end of the round, you make the joining slip stitch into the top of the first half-treble stitch, ignoring the chain-two stitch and continue as before.

At the end of every round, join the round and chain two stitches.

Foundation chain: using colour A, ch 19

Round 1: (ch 2) 3htr in 3rd stitch from hook, htr 17, 3htr in next st, turn 180 degrees to work along the other side of the chain, htr 17. Sl st into 1st htr to join round.

Fasten off (see Fastening off) (40 sts)

Round 2: using colour B in the 3rd loop only (see Making the htr knit stitch) (ch 2, 2htr) in same st, 2htr in next st, 2htr in next st, htr 17, (2htr in next st) x 3, htr 17. Sl st into 1st htr to join round. Fasten off (46 sts)

Round 3: using colour A in the 3rd loop only, (ch 2, 2htr) in same st, htr 1, (2htr in next st, htr 1) x 2, htr 17, (2htr in next st, htr 1) x 3, htr 17. Sl st into 1st htr to join round. Fasten off (52 sts)

Round 4: using colour B in the 3rd loop only, (ch 2, 2htr) in same st, htr 1 in next st, (2htr in next st, htr 1) x 3, 2htr in next st, htr 17, (2htr in next st, htr 1) x 4, 2htr in next st, htr 17. Sl st into 1st htr to join round. Fasten off (62 sts)

Round 5: using colour A in the 3rd loop only, (ch 2, 2htr) in same st, htr 1, (2htr in next st, htr 1) x 6, htr 17, (2htr in next st, htr 1) x 7, htr 17. Sl st into 1st htr to join round. Fasten off (76 sts)

Round 6: using colour B in the 3rd loop only, (ch 2), htr 76

Round 7: using colour A in the 3rd loop only, (ch 2, htr 1) in same st, htr 1, 2htr in next st, (htr 2, 2htr in next st) x 6, htr 17, (htr 2, 2htr in next st) x 7, htr 17. Sl st into 1st htr to join round. Fasten off (90 sts)

Round 8: using colour B in the 3rd loop only, (ch 2), htr 90. Fasten off

Round 9: using colour A in the 3rd loop only, (ch 2, htr 1) in same st, htr 2, 2htr in next st, (htr 3, 2htr in next st) x 6, htr 17, (htr 3, 2htr in next st) x 7, htr 17. Sl st into 1st htr to join round. Fasten off (104 sts)

Round 10: using colour B in the 3rd loop only, (ch 2), htr 104. Fasten off

Round 11: using colour A in the 3rd loop only, (ch 2, htr 1) in same st, htr 3, 2htr in next st, (htr 4, 2htr in next st) x 6, htr 17, (htr 4, 2htr in next st) x 7, htr 17. Sl st into 1st htr to join round. Fasten off (118 sts)

Round 12: using colour B, (ch 2), htr 118. Fasten off

Round 13: (ch 1, dc 1) in same st, dc 117 in 3rd loop only

Round 14: (ch 1, dc 1) in same st, dc 117.
Fasten off.

MAKING UP

Turn your bathmat so that the wrong side (WS) is facing and sort out all those ends, weaving them nicely out of the way.

Troubleshooting

T-shirt yarn is terrible for being different thicknesses (even within the same bobbin). As a result the curved edges of your bathmat may refuse to lie flat as you are working. Don't worry, If your edges are becoming ruffle-like, then you have too many stitches in that round – try leaving out some (or all) of the increases (these are where you put two half-treble stitches in the same stitch). If your edges are curling upwards, you don't have enough stitches, so add a few increases around the curved edges, every two or three stitches and that will help. Another trick is to use a slightly smaller hook if you find yourself faced with a thick section of yarn.

CHART

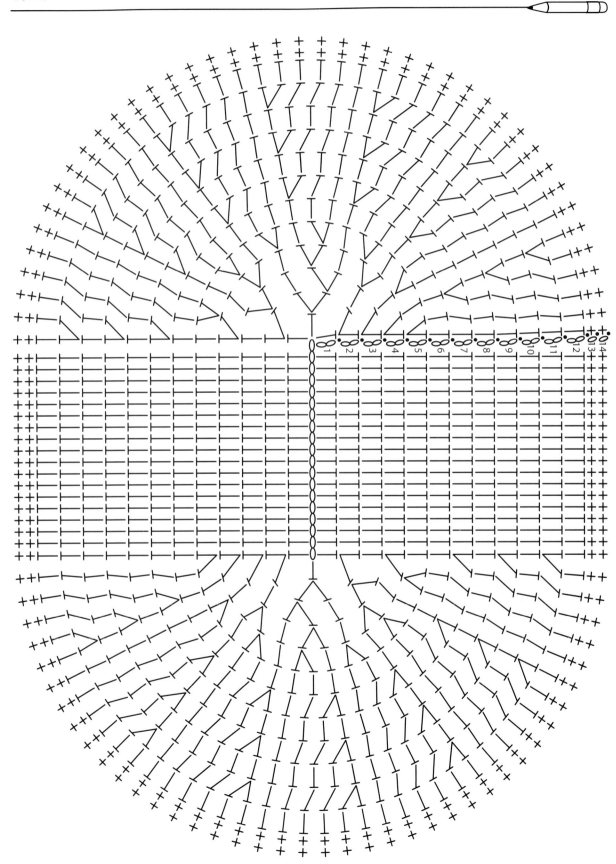

MAHOOOSIVE CLOUD CUSHION

A big cushion, made with big yarn and a big hook. What could be better? This cushion uses the same technique as Little Hearts (see Little Hearts); two identical pieces double crocheted together. Despite its size, this project is a fairly quick make. It needs a lot of filling though!

YOU WILL NEED

I have used...

- 3 x bobbins Hoooked Zpaghetti in Blue and 1 x bobbin of White
- 4 x pillows for stuffing (check they meet current safety standards)

You could use...

- Any extreme yarn and hook to match

You will also need...

- 15mm (US approx. 15 N/P – Q) hook
- Tapestry needle

Finished size:

106 x 55cm (41¾ x 21¾in) tall

PATTERN

(Make 2)

At the beginning of each row, chain one and turn your work.

Foundation chain: in blue, (loosely) ch 58

The right side (RS) of your work is when the tail from the foundation chain is on the left side.

Row 1: (ch1), dc 58
Row 2: dc 57, 2dc in last st (59 sts)
Row 3: 2dc in first st, dc 58 (60 sts)
Row 4: dc 59, 2dc in last st (61 sts)
Row 5: 2dc in first st, dc 60 (62 sts)
Row 6: dc2tog, dc 60 (61 sts)
Row 7: 2dc in first st, dc 60 (62 sts)
Row 8: dc2tog, dc 60 (61 sts)
Row 9: dc 61
Row 10: dc 60, 2dc in last st (62 sts)
Row 11: dc 60, dc2tog (61 sts)
Row 12a: dc2tog, dc 7, dc2tog (9 sts)
Row 13a: dc2tog, dc 5, dc2tog (7 sts)
Row 14a: dc2tog, dc 3, dc2tog (5 sts)
Fasten off (see Fastening off).

Don't turn your work. Put the yarn on your hook with a slip knot (see Making a slip knot).

With wrong side (WS) facing, insert your hook in the stitch on row 11 right next to the bump, and continue working from right to left.

Row 12: dc2tog, dc 48 (49 sts)
Row 13–16: dc 49
Row 17: dc 47, dc2tog (48 sts)
Rows 18–20: dc 48
Row 21: dc2tog, dc 44, dc2tog (46 sts)
Row 22: dc 44, dc2tog (45 sts)
Row 23: dc2tog, dc 43 (44 sts)
Row 24: dc2tog, dc 40, dc2tog (42 sts)
Row 25a: dc2tog, dc 5, dc2tog (7 sts)
Row 26a: dc2tog, dc 3, dc2tog (5 sts)
Fasten off.

The pattern continues to make the next 'bump' on the left side. Turn your work so the RS is facing. Put the yarn on your hook with a slip knot.

Insert your hook in the stitch on row 24, right next to the bump on the right, and continue working from right to left. This next row works straight across to the left side, ready for the next bump.

Row 25: dc2tog, dc 32 (33 sts)
Row 26b: dc2tog, dc 8, dc2tog (10 sts)
Row 27b: dc2tog, dc 6, dc2tog (8 sts)
Row 28b: dc2tog, dc 4, dc2tog (6 sts)
Fasten off.

Don't turn your work. Put the yarn on your hook with a slip knot.

With WS facing, insert your hook in the stitch on row 25, right next to the bump you've just made, and continue working from right to left.

Rows 26–32: dc 20 (20 sts)
Row 33: dc2tog, dc 16, dc2tog (18 sts)
Row 34: dc 18
Row 35: dc2tog, dc 14, dc2tog (16 sts)
Row 36: dc2tog, dc 12, dc2tog (14 sts)
Row 37: dc2tog, dc 10, dc2tog (12 sts)
Row 38: dc2tog, dc 8, dc2tog (10 sts)
Row 39: dc2tog, dc 6, dc2tog (8 sts)
Fasten off.

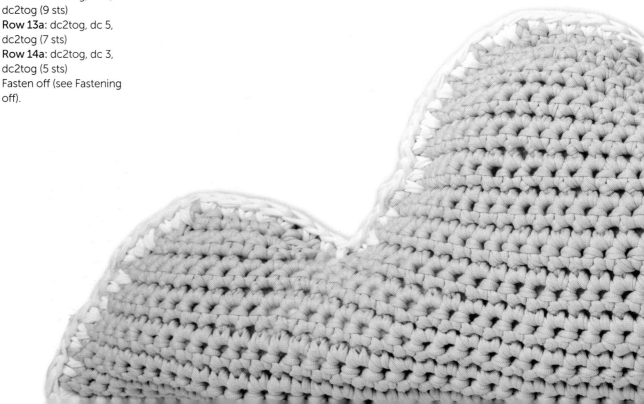

MAKING UP

First of all, you've got to deal with any joins you made. This couldn't be easier. Decide which will be the front piece of the cushion and knot together all the ends on the reverse side — you can easily pull the ends through from the front. You don't need to weave in the ends as they'll be hidden inside the cushion. Now, on the other cushion piece, knot together all the ends on the front side. Again, these will all be hidden inside the cushion.

Now you need to crochet the two pieces together. With the white yarn, put a slip knot on your hook and just as you did with the hearts (see Little Hearts), insert the hook through a stitch near the edge of both cloud pieces. I started on the right edge of my cushion. Yarn over and make a double crochet stitch. Continue around the cloud, making double crochet stitches through the stitches at the very edge of both the pieces.

Remember to stuff the pillow quite firmly before finishing off your double crochets around the edge and fasten off. Weave in ends (see Weaving in ends).

All that's left to do is for you to find somewhere to keep your rather large cushion!

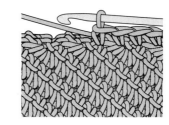

OTHER THINGS TO TRY

You can always down-scale this cushion by making it in a regular double knit yarn. It will obviously be much smaller.

FANCY
STITCHES

There are lots of different ways to mix and match the stitches you already know to create patterns and shapes. Some of these lend themselves well to repetition and are perfect for blankets, cushions, scarves and shawls, whilst adding texture and interest to your projects.

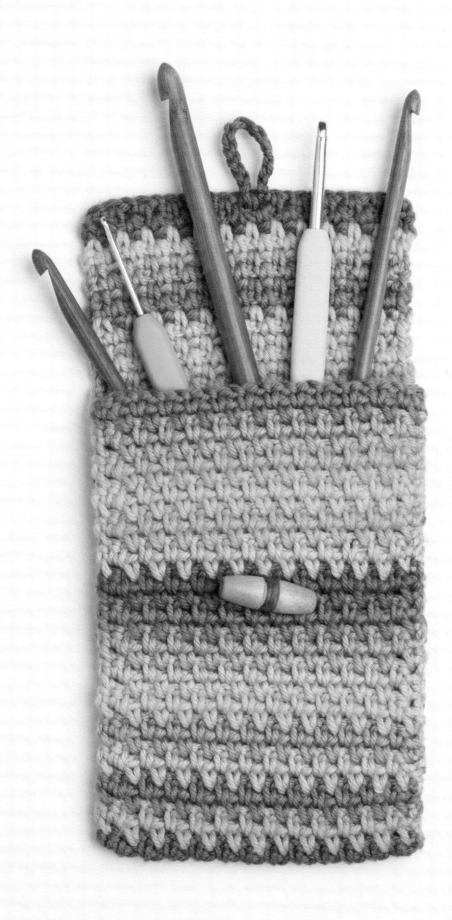

MOSS STITCH

This is quite a greedy little stitch as it also likes to be known as 'granite stitch', 'linen stitch' and 'woven stitch' too. It's striking and adds texture to your work plus its really easy! It's based on ...wait for it ... a double crochet stitch and a chain stitch. I told you it was easy. This means that it still produces a fairly dense stitch that is perfect for cushions, cosies, hats and scarves. And the spiky stitch effect looks really effective in lots of stripy colour changes as well as in a solid block of colour.

CHART

It's very easy to see the alternating patterns of double crochet and chain stitch along the rows. The double crochet is made into the chain-one space, which makes an overlapping pattern. You'll see at the beginning of row 2, and all other even rows, you need to make two double crochet stitches to make the pattern work.

Foundation chain: ch 15

Row 1: (ch 1) dc 1, *ch 1, sk st, dc 1* repeat across row

1. Make your chain stitch, work back along the foundation chain and put the first double crochet in the second stitch from the hook. Then chain one, skip a stitch and put another double crochet in the following stitch (see arrows on illustration). Repeat this along.

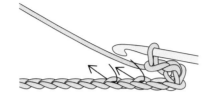

Row 2: (ch 1, turn) dc 1, dc 1 in ch-1sp, *ch 1, dc 1 in ch-1 sp* repeat across row, dc 1 in final stitch

1. This is similar to row 1, make your first double crochet in the second stitch from the hook, and then make the next double crochet in the chain-one space. Chain one, then make one double crochet in the following chain-one space (see arrow on illustration). Repeat along the row, ending with another double crochet in the final stitch.

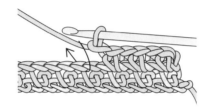

Row 3: (ch 1, turn) dc 1, ch 1, *dc 1 in ch-1 sp, ch 1* repeat across row, and dc 1 in final stitch

Rows 4 onwards: Repeat rows 2 and 3 alternately

CHANGING THE COLOURS

There's nothing too tricky about this, but it can feel a little fiddly to begin with as you're going to change colour in the last stitch of the row – don't worry, it doesn't show. Crochet along the row as usual. When you reach the final double crochet stitch, do the following:

1. Insert hook into the stitch as usual, yarn over and pull the yarn through. You'll have two loops on the hook.

2. Hold the old colour tail and the new colour tail together with your right hand, behind your work.

3. Yarn over in the new colour and complete the stitch.

4. Chain one for the next row, turn and continue the pattern as usual.

5. Remember to cut the old yarn and tie the ends together.

If you think you've cracked it, then let's move on to the project. It's a Moss/Granite/Linen/Woven stitch fiesta.

A CASE FOR A GADGET

What shall I crochet around next? Aha! My e-book reader. It looks very dull when I'm not using it, very dull indeed. And it could get scratched in my bag. Crocheted in different coloured rows of the fabulous moss/granite/linen/woven stitch, this striking case will keep your gadget clean, warm and unscratched. The case is made as one long rectangle and stitched together along the sides. The opening of this case is secured with a toggle. You can use any interesting button for this, or attach the fastening of your choice.

YOU WILL NEED

I have used...

• 1 x 50g ball Debbie Bliss Cotton DK in: Teal (shade 39), Denim (shade 51), Aqua (shade 61), Periwinkle (shade 62), Gold (shade 63), Peach (shade 65), Lavender (shade 66), Lilac (shade 67)

You could use...

• Any DK, Aran or Worsted weight yarn and hook to match.

You will also need...

• 4mm (US 6/G) hook
• Tapestry needle
• Toggle/ button for fastening

Finished size:

12 x 19cm (4½ x 7¼in)

PATTERN

Work in rows.

Foundation chain: ch 25
Row 1: (ch 1) dc 1, *ch 1, sk st, dc 1* repeat across row
At the beginning of every row, chain one and turn your work.

Row 2: (ch 1, turn) dc 1, dc 1 in ch-1sp, *ch 1, dc 1 in ch-1 sp* repeat across row and dc 1 in final stitch

Row 3: change colour, (ch 1, turn) dc 1, ch 1, *dc 1 in ch-1 sp, ch 1* repeat across row, and dc 1 in final stitch
Rows 4–78: Repeat rows 2 and 3 alternately. Change colour every two rows.
Fasten off (see Fastening off).

Adjusting the pattern

Measure the width of your gadget and make the foundation chain approximately the same. The foundation chain must be an odd number of stitches for the pattern to work. Add more or fewer rows to fit the length of your gadget.

OTHER THINGS TO TRY

You can adapt this pattern to make a cushion cover in exactly the same way; increase the foundation chain to fit the width of the cushion (make sure it is an odd number of stitches) and crochet enough rows to go around the cushion and make a flap. Stitch it along the sides and attach buttons to secure it. Easy.

MAKING UP

This gadget case is designed to fold over twice. Once to cover the entire gadget front and back and again over the top of the gadget to provide a flap so you can get your device in and out.

1. If you've changed colour every two rows as I did, then you will notice rather a lot of ends that need weaving in. Make sure that you weave them in what will be the inside of the case.

2. To stitch the sides together, choose one of the colours (I used Lavender) and sew carefully along the sides, catching stitches from one side and securing them to the other. Fasten off and weave in ends (see Weaving in ends).

3. Attach the button or fastening. Choose another colour of yarn and sew the button in place on the main section of the case.

4. To make the button loop, crochet a chain long enough to fit (mine is 10 stitches), leaving a 10cm (4in) tail at either end for sewing to the flap. Sew in place, fasten off and weave in ends.

STITCH TUTORIAL:
BOBBLE STITCH

Bobble stitches add a spot of fun to your crochet and will make the texture of your items a little more interesting. Bobbles can be used right next to each other, or spaced out for effect. They are created by cramming together lots of treble crochet stitches until they pop out of your work. The surrounding stitches are usually short (like double crochet) to make the bobble more noticeable. There are lots of different bobble stitches out there; the popcorn stitch and the puff stitch are both different versions.

Are you ready to get all puffed-up? Get your practise yarn and hook and let's do it!

CHART

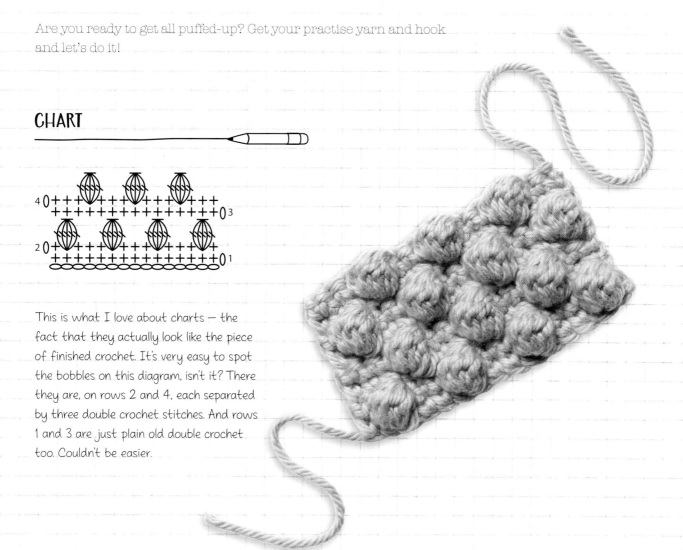

This is what I love about charts — the fact that they actually look like the piece of finished crochet. It's very easy to spot the bobbles on this diagram, isn't it? There they are, on rows 2 and 4, each separated by three double crochet stitches. And rows 1 and 3 are just plain old double crochet too. Couldn't be easier.

Foundation chain: ch 15

Row 1: (ch 1) dc 15

Row 2: (ch 1, turn) dc 1, bobble in next st, *dc 3, bobble in next st* repeat along the row. Dc 1 in final stitch

1. Chain one and turn your work. Make one double crochet in the second stitch from your hook.

2. Yarn over hook and insert hook in the stitch. Yarn over and pull it through the stitch. Yarn over and pull through the first two loops (two loops on hook)

3. Repeat step 2 (three loops on hook)

4. Repeat step 2 (four loops on hook)

5. Repeat step 2 (five loops on hook)

6. Repeat step 2 (six loops on hook)

7. Yarn over and pull through all six loops and tighten slightly.

8. Now make three double crochet stitches to separate the bobbles and put another bobble stitch in the following stitch.

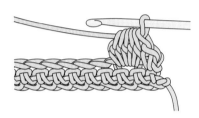

9. Continue the pattern across the row, ending with a double crochet in the last stitch. You will have four bobbles in this row.

10. As the bobbles always ends up on the side facing away from you, the next row will just be a plain row of double crochet.

Row 3: (ch 1, turn) dc 15

Row 4: (ch 1, turn) dc 3, *bobble in next st, dc 3* repeat along the row.

1. Chain one and turn, then make three double crochet stitches. In the next stitch, make the bobble stitch as before. Repeat this across the row and you'll have three bobbles in this row.

Row 5 and beyond: repeat rows 1–4

BOBBLY HEADWARMER

Some days I want a hat. Other days I just want to keep the chill away from my ears. For those days, a headwarmer is just the ticket. Crocheted in alternate rows of half-treble crochet and bobble stitches, this funky little number will help you practise those puffy little balls.

YOU WILL NEED

I have used...
- 1 x 50g ball Debbie Bliss Cashmerino Aran in Gold (shade 63)

You could use...
- Any DK, Aran or Worsted weight yarn, with some wool content for warmth, and hook to match.

You will also need...
- 5.5mm (US 9/I) hook
- Tapestry needle

Finished size:
9.5 x 50cm (3¾ x 9½in)

PATTERN

To make the bobble stitch: tr5tog in same stitch.

Foundation chain: ch 72
Row 1: (ch 3 counts as tr), tr 72 (73 sts)

Remember that the ch 2 at the beginning of every row is the turning chain and is not counted as a stitch.

Row 2: (ch 2, turn) htr 12, bobble in next st, *htr 5, bobble in next st* repeat x 8 (9 bobbles in total), htr 12
Row 3: (ch 2, turn) htr 73

Row 4: (ch 2, turn) htr 15, bobble in next st, *htr 5, bobble in next st* repeat x 7 (8 bobbles in total), htr 15
Row 5: Repeat row 3
Row 6: Repeat row 2
Row 7: Repeat row 3
Row 8: Repeat row 4
Row 9: Repeat row 2
Row 10: Repeat row 3
Row 11: (ch 3 counts as tr, turn) tr 72 (73 sts)
Fasten off (see Fastening off). Leave a 50cm (19½in) tail for sewing together.

MAKING UP

Thread the long tail onto the tapestry needle and sew the short edges of the headwarmer together. You can use a whip stitch or freestyle across the stitches — so long as your seam is secure, you can do as you please. As you are using the same coloured yarn your stitches won't be visible.

Adjusting the pattern

This pattern has the bobble motif in the middle section of the rows, sandwiched between half-treble stitches. To adjust the pattern, you just need to alter the number of half-treble stitches made either side of the bobble pattern. For example, let's make the pattern 5cm (2in) larger. To do this, I'm going to add four stitches to each side of the pattern (eight stitches in total). First, I'll increase the foundation chain by eight to give a total of 80 stitches. Then I'll add four more to the half-treble stitches at the beginning and end of rows 2 and 4.

The pattern would read something like this:

Row 2: (ch 2, turn) htr 16, bobble in next st, *htr 5, bobble in next st* repeat x 8 (9 bobbles in total), htr 16
Row 4: (ch 2, turn) htr 19, bobble in next st, *htr 5, bobble in next st* repeat x 7 (8 bobbles in total), htr 19

Apply exactly the same principle to make the headwarmer smaller, too. Just make sure you add or subtract an equal number of stitches from either side of the pattern and Bob's your uncle.

OTHER THINGS TO TRY

The bobble stitch is great for all sorts of projects. How about making a much, much longer version of this for a scarf? All you'd need to do is repeat the middle bobble section six or seven times and perhaps add a few more rows and you'd have a matching headwarmer and scarf set!

STITCH ON THE EDGE

The perfect edging can finish off your work beautifully. Edging can also be an important part of shaping some projects and can help tidy up uneven sides. Edging can be very simple (think rows of double crochet) or exquisitely ornamental with complicated combinations of stitches. Edging can be used around all sides of a crocheted item, or just one, depending on what you are making. You can use one stitch repeated across several rows, or go for a mixture of different layers. The most important thing is that the edging is made using the same type of yarn as the project, otherwise you could risk misshaping it, or it might do something strange in the wash.

Let's keep things simple and learn four basic patterns before launching into the projects.

To practise these edges, you need something to crochet around, so why not knock up a few samples to use? (I've used a foundation chain of 15, then five rows of double crochet stitches.)

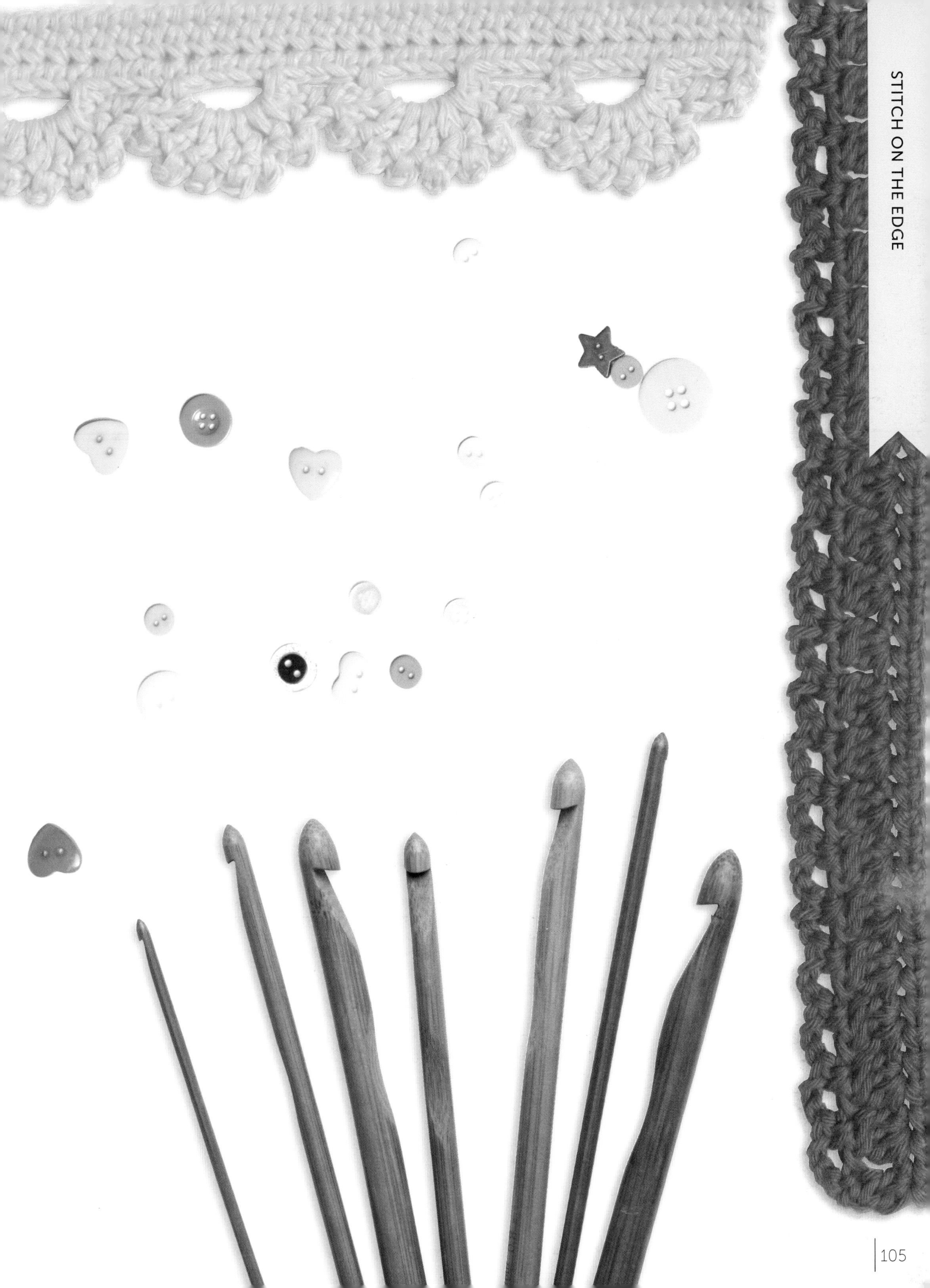

BASIC EDGING

DOUBLE CROCHET EDGE

You've already mastered this little beauty,
but here's a reminder of the basic principles:

CHART

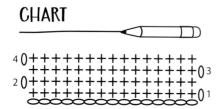

> You can make this
> edging just the once,
> or repeat with several
> rows or rounds.

Double crochet row: dc across all stitches.

1. Have your work with right side (RS) facing you. Put the yarn onto your hook with a slipknot (see Making a slip knot) and decide where you are going to begin.

2. Insert your hook into the stitch of your choice and make the double crochet stitch in the usual way (see Stitch tutorial: Working through the chain and double crochet stitch).

3. Continue working across, making a double crochet stitch in every stitch and around your piece from right to left, or anticlockwise if you are working around.

4. If you are negotiating a corner, then make three double crochets in the corner stitch.

5. Once you've completed the row or round, fasten off (see Fastening off) and weave in the ends (see Weaving in ends).

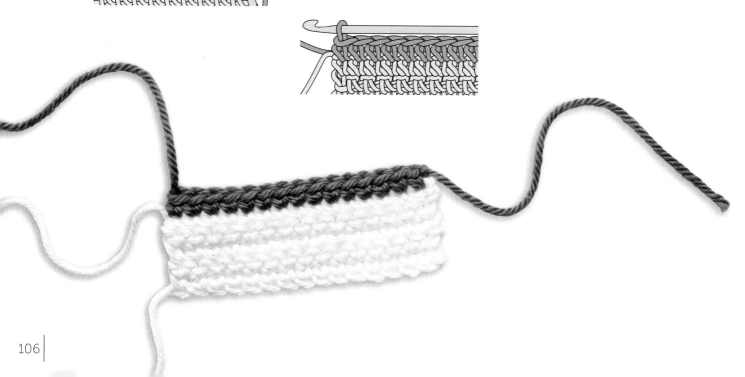

PICOT EDGE

A picot stitch is based on a chain stitch. Picot stitches are added to the top of a stitch:

CHART

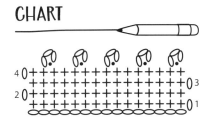

Picot stitch is another fiddly manoeuvre. Try rolling your hook gently from side to side to ease through the stitches.

Picot row: dc 2, picot, *dc 3, picot* across, dc 1 in final st

1. Have your work with RS facing you. Put the yarn onto your hook with a slipknot and decide where you are going to begin. Insert your hook into the stitch of your choice and make two double crochet stitches.

2. Now for the picot. Chain three and insert your hook through the third chain from the hook.

3. Yarn over and pull the yarn through all the stitch. One picot stitch made!

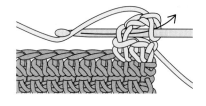

4. Follow the picot stitch with three double crochet stitches, then another picot. Continue this pattern across, ending with one double crochet in the last stitch.

SCALLOP EDGE

The scallop shape is achieved by making lots of treble crochet stitches in one stitch, with a short double crochet stitch either side to achieve the shaping. It works best when worked into a row of existing double crochet stitches. Make sure the wrong side (WS) of your work is facing you, and then make a row of double crochet. Turn your work so the RS is facing you to make the scallop stitches:

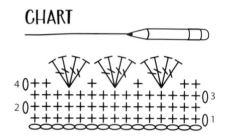

CHART

Scallop row: dc 2, *sk st, 4tr in next st, sk st, dc 1 * repeat across, dc 1 in final st

1. Have your work with RS facing you. Put the yarn onto your hook with a slipknot and decide where you are going to begin. Insert your hook into the stitch of your choice and make one double crochet stitch, then another.

2. Now skip a stitch and make four treble crochet stitches (the scallop) in the next stitch.

3. Skip a stitch and make one double crochet in the next stitch. Repeat from step 2 across the row, ending with one double crochet in the last stitch.

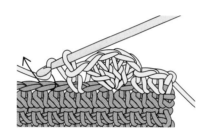

Scallop stitches create a pretty edging and can vary in the number of treble crochets they contain, as well as the number of stitches skipped between them.

RUFFLE EDGE

Ruffles can add a bit of volume to the edges of a blanket or cushion.
They are ridiculously easy, just several tall stitches in every stitch.

CHART

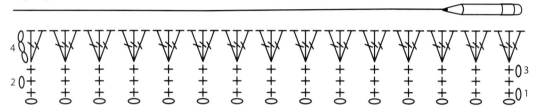

Ruffle Row: ch 3 (counts as tr), 2tr in same st, 3tr in every stitch.

1. Have your work with RS facing you. Put the yarn onto your hook with a slipknot and decide where you are going to begin. Insert your hook into the stitch of your choice and make a chain of three. This counts as the first treble crochet stitch.

2. Put two more treble crochet stitches in the same stitch to make three in total.

3. Make three treble crochet stitches in each stitch across the row.

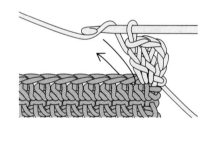

This edging can be made as ruffle-tastic as you like, depending on how many treble crochet stitches you want to squeeze into each stitch; more trebles equals a more voluptuous ruffle.

BOOT CUFFS

These bootcuffs are crocheted in a ribbed stitch and finished off with a contrasting scallop edge.

I've used two different hook sizes for this project; the smaller hook is for the edging. You can make the whole project using just the 6mm (US 10/J) hook and it will still work beautifully.

YOU WILL NEED

I have used...

- 2 x 50g balls Debbie Bliss Blue Faced Leicester Aran in Duck Egg (shade 14)
- 1 x 50g ball Debbie Bliss Blue Faced Leicester Aran in Mustard (shade 06)

You could use...

- Any DK, Aran or Worsted weight yarn and hook to match.

You will also need...

- 6mm (US 10/J) and 5.5mm (US 9/I) hook
- Tapestry needle

Finished size:

32 x 13cm (12½ x 5in)

CHART (edging)

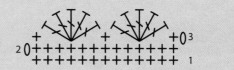

PATTERN

Cuffs

(Make 2)

These boot cuffs are worked sideways to create a vertical ribbed effect.

Work in rows. At the beginning of every row, chain 1 and turn.

Foundation chain: Using 6mm (US 10/J) hook and Duck Egg, ch 25
Row 1: dc 25
Rows 2–56: dc 25 in BLO
Fasten off (see Fastening off), leaving a 50cm (19½in) tail for sewing together.

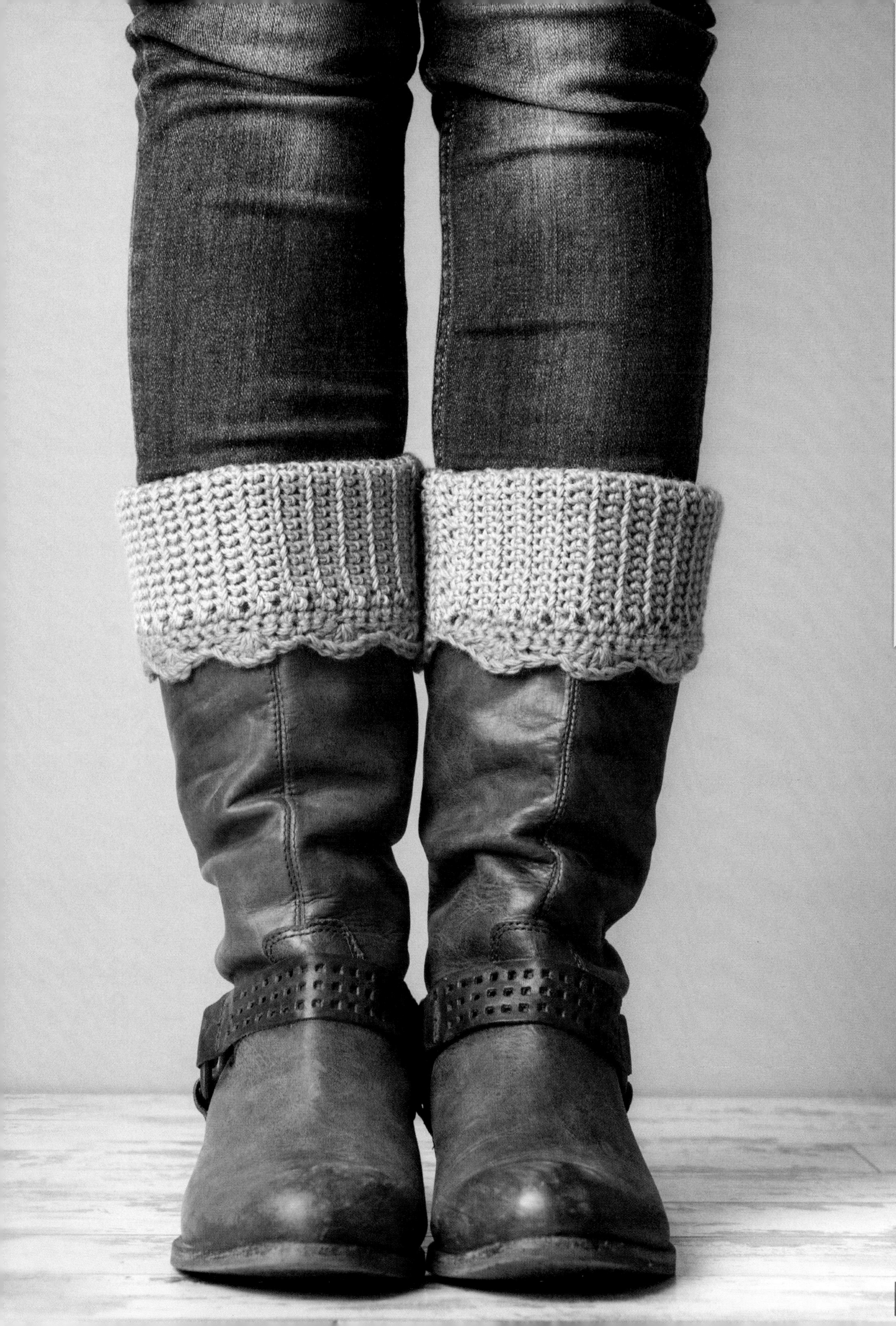

MAKING UP

Have the boot cuff with the RS facing you and turn the short edges into the centre. Thread your tapestry needle with the long yarn tail and stitch across, catching stitches from each side to create a strong seam. Your stitches won't be visible, so don't worry too much. Fasten off and weave in ends (see Weaving in ends).

Turn the boot cuff the right way out and put your crochet hook back into where you finished the edging. Make one or two double crochet stitches to cover the join of the seam with the edging. Fasten off and weave in ends.

Now don your cute boot cuffs and rejoice in the fact that your boots look more stylish and your legs feel more cosy.

Edging

You will work along the long edge of your boot cuff, so turn your piece the right way, with right side (RS) facing you.

Row 1: Using 5.5mm (US 9/I) hook and Mustard, dc 55

Attach the yarn to your hook with a slip knot (see Making a slip knot) and insert the hook into the stitch on the right-hand side at the top of your piece. Yarn over and make your first double crochet stitch.

Work from right to left, making double crochet stitches across the ends of the row. You crocheted 56 rows, so you should be able to make 55 double crochet stitches (it needs to be 55 stitches for the scallop pattern to work).

Row 2: ch 1, turn, dc 55
Row 3: ch 1, turn, dc 1, *sk 2 sts, 5tr in next st, sk 2 sts, dc in next st* repeat across row but don't fasten off just yet (see Making up).

This is the row with the scallop shaping in. Chain one and turn your work, then make one double crochet in the second stitch from your hook.

Skip two stitches and make five treble stitches in the next stitch.

Skip two more stitches and make one double crochet in the following stitch. Repeat the pattern across the row.

Don't fasten off just yet, as you'll finish the edging once the seam is sewn. You could use a stitch marker to hold the final stitch for you, if you like.

Adjusting the pattern

To make the boot cuff longer, increase the foundation chain and all the rows to the length desired. To alter the width of the boot cuff you'll need to adjust the number of rows. The scallop pattern works on a multiple of six stitches and add one more. You can always make extra double crochet stitches at the beginning and end of row 3 of the scallop pattern to help you.

OTHER THINGS TO TRY

You can trim the tops of your boot cuffs with whatever edging you desire. How about trying the picot edging? Or maybe a bit of frilly ruffling is more your thing.

DECORATIVE EDGING

Make your shelves prettier by adding some decorative crochet edging. It's great for hiding chipped edges and grubby finger-prints! These edges are crocheted in rows to the length you desire. Edging doesn't just have to be used for shelves. You could stitch them onto anything that needs a bit of prettifying.

YOU WILL NEED

I have used...
- 1 x 50g ball Rico Creative Cotton Aran in: Candy Pink (shade 64), Orange (shade 74) and Yellow (shade 63)

You could use...
- Any DK weight yarn and hook to match.

You will also need...
- 4mm (US 6/G) hook
- Tapestry needle

Finished sizes:
(Pink) 3.5 x 50cm
(1⅜ x 19½in) long
(Orange) 3.5 x 50cm (1⅜ x 19½in)
(Yellow) 5 x 50cm
(2 x 19½in)

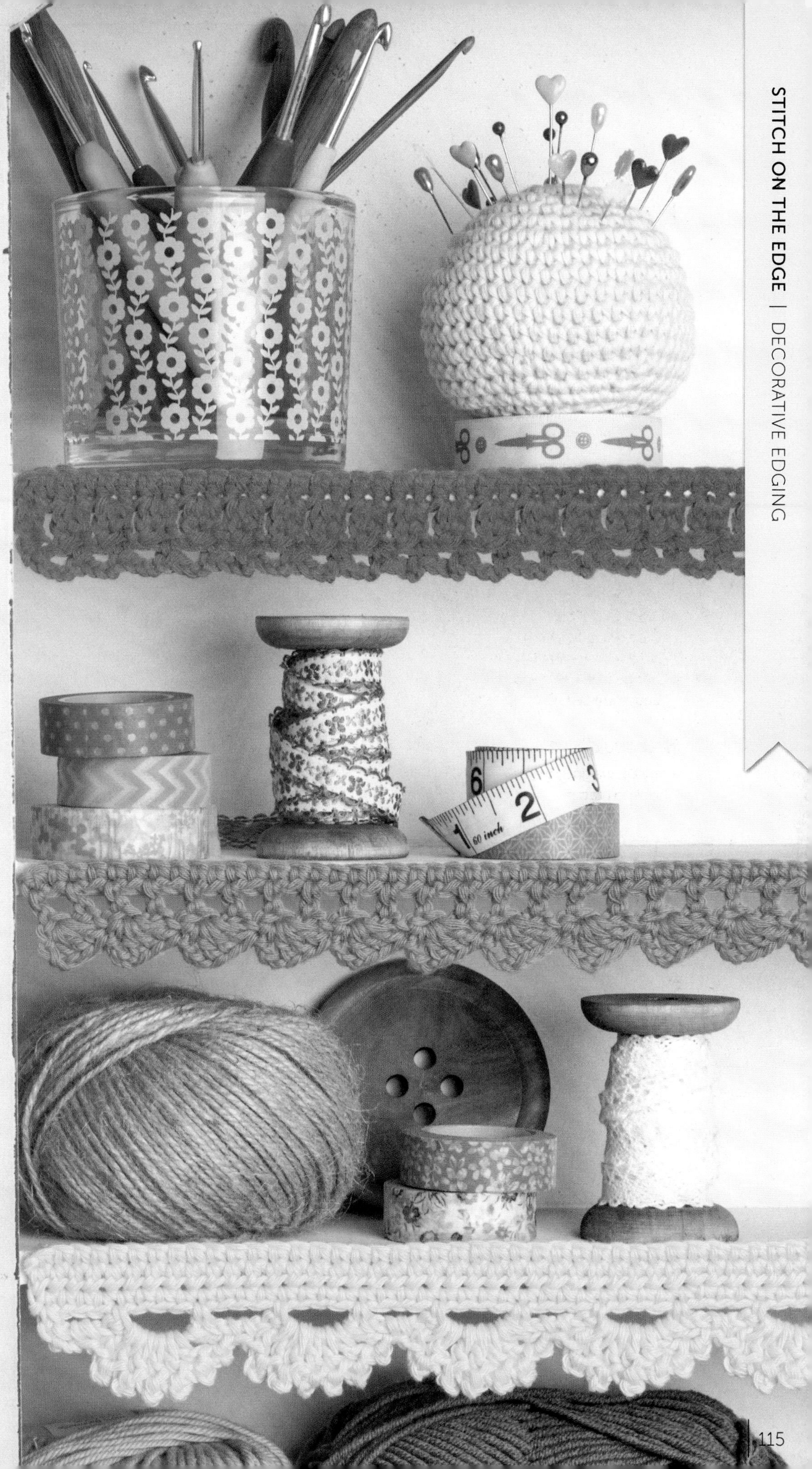
60 inch

PINK EDGING

CHART

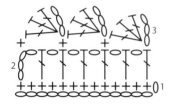

PATTERN

Foundation chain: ch 97 (Multiple of 4 + 1)
Row 1: (ch 1) dc 97
Row 2: (ch 4 (counts as tr and ch 1), turn), tr in 7th st from hook, *ch 1, sk st, tr in next st* repeat across

Row 3: (ch 3, turn) 3tr in same st, sk 3 sts, dc in next st, *ch 3, 3tr in same st, sk 3 sts, dc in next st* repeat across
Fasten off (see Fastening off). Weave in ends (see Weaving in ends).

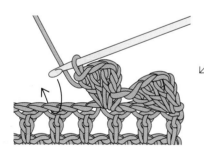

ORANGE EDGING

CHART

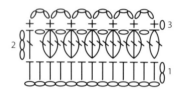

PATTERN

The front of this edging is actually the wrong side (WS), so the beginning tail will be at the bottom right.

Foundation chain: ch 89 (Multiple of 4 +1)
Row 1: (ch 2) htr 89
Row 2: (ch 3, turn) tr 1 in 4th stitch from hook, ch 1, sk st, *tr3tog in next st, ch 1, sk st* repeat along row, tr2tog in last st

Make a chain of three and put a treble crochet in the fourth stitch from the hook. Chain one and skip a stitch. In the next stitch you need to make a treble-crochet-three-together stitch. This is just like the bobble stitch, but with three treble stitches, not five:

Yarn over and insert hook in the stitch. Yarn over and pull it through the stitch. Yarn over and pull yarn through the first two loops (two loops on hook).

Repeat step 1 (three loops on hook).

Repeat step 1 (four loops on hook).

Yarn over and pull through all four loops.

Chain one, skip a stitch and repeat the pattern along the row, ending with a treble-crochet-two-together stitch in the final stitch.

Row 3: (ch 1, turn), dc1, *ch 3, sk st, dc in next st* repeat across row
Fasten off. Weave in ends.

YELLOW EDGING

CHART

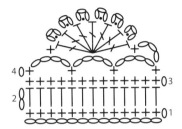

PATTERN

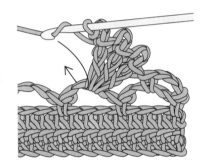

Foundation chain: ch 93
(Multiple of 8 + 5)
Row 1: (ch 1) dc 93
Row 2: (ch 2, turn) htr 93
Row 3: (ch 1, turn) dc 93
Row 4: (ch 1, turn) dc
1, *ch 4, sk 3 sts, dc 1*
repeat across

Row 5: (ch 3, turn) dc
1 in first ch-4 sp, *(6tr
with picot, tr 1) in next
ch-4-sp, dc 1 in next
ch-4 sp* repeat along
row
Fasten off. Weave in
ends.

OTHER THINGS TO TRY

You could decorate the edge of a plain lampshade by attaching one of these borders along the bottom. Or how about adding detail to a skirt or coat? There are no excuses for boring edges anymore!

MAKING UP

It's now just a case of deciding where you want to put your edging. To attach it to shelving, you could use double-sided sticky tape, glue or pin it across. If adding to another piece of fabric, then use your embroidery needle and strong thread to stitch it in place.

Adjusting the patterns

For each pattern, refer back to the Foundation chain instruction. Here, you will see 'Multiple of …' in brackets. This tells you how to calculate the length of the foundation chain – so, for the Pink edging, it says '(Multiple of 4 + 1)', so ensure the starting chain is a multiple of four then add one more.

FINISHING
TOUCHES

You have done it! You have made it to the end of a pattern. You have created a wonderful crocheted item and cannot stop admiring it with a feeling of deep satisfaction and smugness. You are rehearsing the unveiling of your project to friends and family and imagining their awe-struck faces...

...but, oh dear, it's not quite finished. You just need to get rid of those ends and add something pretty, but how?

Never fear, dear reader – everything you need to know is on the next pages. I'll explain how to get your project ship-shape and will soon have you showing off your wonderful crocheted creation to anyone who'll stand still for long enough...

JOINING NEW YARN

1. There are plenty of times when you are crocheting that you'll need to join a bit of new yarn to your work. It might be that you're changing colour, there's a nasty bit in the yarn you've had to cut out or that you've simply come to the end of your yarn ball. Whatever the reason, you need to know how to join a new bit to an old bit.

2. When you're making a crochet stitch, there is a point in its construction (just before the final yarn over and completing the stitch) when you have two loops left on the hook.* This is when the joining of new yarn needs to happen!

3. Hold the old yarn tail out of the way and the new yarn tail in your right hand.

4. Yarn over in the new colour and pull through to complete the stitch. Cleverly, this method finishes the old stitch in the old colour and the new yarn is ready for the next stitch.

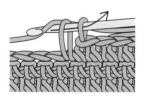 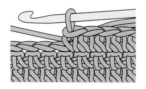

5. Make a few more stitches.

6. Pull the yarn tails gently to tighten the stitches, cut the old yarn tail and knot to the new yarn tail.

7. Weave away the tails when you finish off.

* When making half-treble stitches, you never have two loops on your hook, only three at this same point.

CHANGING COLOUR AT THE END OF A ROW

Use this method if you want to change the colour for the next row. Crochet along the row as usual, making your stitches as directed. When you reach the final crochet stitch, make the colour change to complete the stitch. Make the turning chain as directed and continue with the following row in the new colour. After a few stitches, cut the old yarn and knot the tails together. Weave in the ends when you're ready to finish off.

ADDING NEW YARN WHEN YOU'VE FASTENED OFF

This method is useful when you want to add decorative edging, or if you're working on a motif in joined rounds. So, imagine that you've completed a round or edge and fastened off. Now you want to add another row/ round. There are two different methods you can try:

STARTING WITH TYING THE YARN TAILS TOGETHER

1. This can be used when you're starting the new round right next to where you've finished the last round – when making granny squares, for example.

2. Cut the yarn, leaving a 10cm (4in) tail and pull it through the final stitch, fastening off. Now knot this end together with your new colour, at the back of your work, as close to the stitches as you can.

3. Insert your hook in the place where you will make your first stitch, yarn over in the new colour and pull the yarn through the space.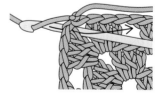

4. Yarn over and make the chain stitches needed. Continue with the pattern for that row/round.

STARTING WITH A SLIP KNOT

1. This can be used when there is no yarn end to knot your new yarn to, for example when adding edging.

2. Put the new yarn onto your hook with a slip knot.

3. Insert your hook wherever you are going to begin the new row/round.

4. Yarn over and pull the yarn through the stitch.

5. Either yarn over again and pull the yarn through both loops to make a double crochet stitch...

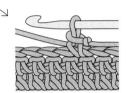

6. ...or pull this yarn through the loop on your hook too, to make a slip stitch (you'll need to do this if you're going to be working with taller stitches and need to make a chain first).

FASTENING OFF

Cut your yarn, leaving a tail of 15cm (6in) and pull it through your final stitch. This is known as fastening off.

WEAVING IN ENDS

Now you need to hide the tails!

Begin by deciding which is the front side of your work, thread the yarn end onto your tapestry needle and sew it through some of the stitches on the reverse. Carefully snip the end away and repeat for any other tails. This is known as weaving in the ends.

CHANGING COLOUR IN CONTINUOUS ROUNDS OF DOUBLE CROCHET
(e.g. when toy making)

You can change yarn when working in continuous rounds, but you will notice a slight stepping of the colours. It doesn't really matter – just make sure that your colour changes are all at the back- this might be in the middle of a round so use your stitch marker to remind you where the first stitch of the round is. All you need to do is change colour as above but make the next stitch following the colour change a slip stitch, not a double crochet stitch. What this does is lower the height of the stitch and make the colour join less obvious. Carry on as usual and treat the slip stitch as an ordinary stitch when you return to it on the following row.

And that's how it's done. None of the methods are difficult – they will just need a little practise to perfect.

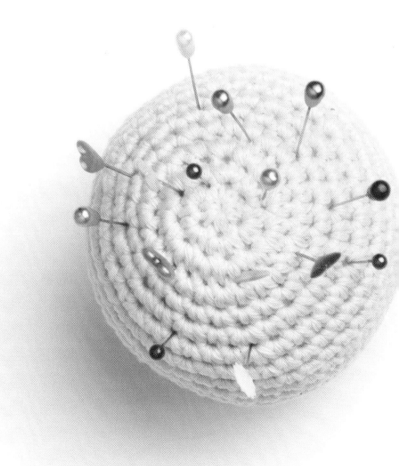

BLOCKING

Blocking is a technique to gently ease projects into shape. It helps to define the stitches, making them look sharper and stops pesky curling. For an item that is worn, such as a shawl, it can relax the stitches and improve the drape of the garment. Generally, yarns made from natural fibres work best, but synthetics can be blocked, too.

Not everything you crochet needs blocking. However, there are times when you'll want to block and you'll need to know how.

There are a few different methods for blocking, but the essential premise is that you are pinning your crochet into shape, making it damp, and allowing it to dry. The two methods I'll show you are wet blocking and steam blocking.

WET BLOCKING

YOU WILL NEED

- Piece of completed crochet (all fibres)
- Rust-proof pins
- A suitable surface (choose from the following – blocking board, ironing board, foam mats/cork mat/carpet covered in towels – all will do the job nicely)
- Spray bottle filled with warm water or
- Spray starch (see below)

HOW TO WET BLOCK

1. Pin your crocheted item onto the suitable surface to the desired shape. Make sure the pins are evenly spaced around the edges and pull the crochet gently.

2. Gently spray with spray starch or just warm water – you want the crochet damp, but not soaking.

3. Leave to dry completely. This can take hours and hours, so make sure it's left somewhere safely away from the cat/dog/kids/spouse.

4. Remove the pins and marvel at your cleverness. You should have a flat, perfectly shaped piece of crochet!

Spray starch or warm water?

This just depends on the finish you're after. If you want something to be quite stiff, like the bunting or shelf edging, then spray starch is the stuff for the job. Otherwise, use warm water.

STEAM BLOCKING

YOU WILL NEED

- Piece of completed crochet (cotton, linen or wool)
- Rust-proof pins with metal head
- A suitable blocking surface
- Iron with steam setting

HOW TO STEAM BLOCK

1. Warning! I would advise that you test a small swatch of your crochet first to make sure nothing untoward happens in the heating process. The last thing you want is a melted mess on your hands. And do please be careful with the iron. Keep dogs, cats, kids and spouses at a safe distance and watch your fingers.

2. Heat the iron to the steam setting. Once it's puffing out steam nicely, it's ready.

3. As before, shape the crocheted item and pin it out evenly onto the suitable surface.

4. Gently hover the iron above your work, pressing the button to release steam evenly across the surface. Too much heat can ruin the yarn, so I'll say it again, be careful.

5. Leave to dry somewhere out of harm's way.

6. Remove the pins and you're done.

And that, in a nutshell is how to block. It's up to you to decide whether your crochet will benefit from it, but it's worth having a try.

EMBELLISHMENTS

Crochet lends itself really well to having all sorts of knick-knacks added to it; buttons, ribbons and trimmings can all finish off a piece beautifully, or hide a mistake. Some embellishments can be glued in place (a favourite quick-fix method of mine), but if your item needs to be washed, worn or cuddled, then you'll need to know how to stitch things in place.

YOU WILL NEED

- Embellishments of your choice
- Embroidery needle
- Embroidery thread
- Sewing thread
- Pins

A WORD ABOUT THREADS

Embroidery thread is often multi-stranded and comes in a variety of thicknesses and sheens. Sewing thread is often made from cotton and/or polyester and is a single, thin strand. Embroidery threads are good for adding decorative stitching as they are slightly thicker. Sewing threads are great for adding delicate, light stitching to secure items together.

SEWING BUTTONS

1. You have two choices here. You can either sew the button using the same yarn that you have made the item in, or with the thread of your choice.

2. Cut a length of thread about 70cm (27½in) and tie a knot in one end.

3. Thread the other end onto your embroidery needle.

4. Position the button in place with your left hand.

5. Carefully bring the needle up through one of the holes in the button and pull gently, but firmly, until you reach the knot.

6. Now pass the needle down though another hole (some buttons have four).

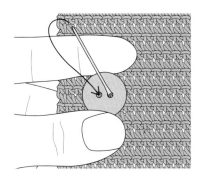

7. Bring the needle up through the first hole and down through the second again.

8. Repeat this a few times until the button feels secure.

9. Turn your work to the back and pass the needle through one of the stitches to form a loop. Bring your needle back through this loop and tighten to form a knot. Repeat this twice more to secure the thread and snip the ends carefully away.

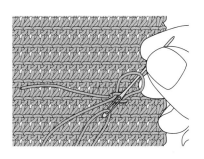

SEWING TRIM

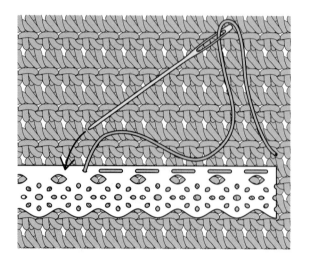

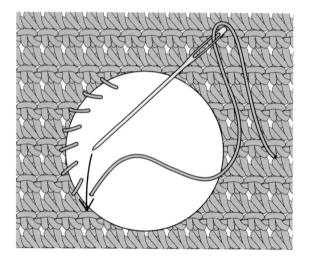

RUNNING STITCH FOR RIBBON/ EDGING

1. As before, decide on the thread you would like to use. If you want the stitching to be almost invisible then choose sewing thread in a matching colour to your trim. If you are stitching a wide trim, then you may want to make two rows of stitches, one along the top edge and one along the bottom.

2. Cut a length of thread long enough to fix the trimming and tie a knot in one end (you can always cut more thread, so don't worry too much).

3. Thread the other end onto your embroidery needle.

4. Position the trim and carefully hold or pin in place.

5. Starting at one end, bring the needle up through the crochet and the trim and pull gently, but firmly, until you reach the knot.

6. Now make a short stitch (the length is really up to you) by passing the needle back down though the trim.

7. Bring the needle up again and make another stitch. Try to keep the stitches and the spaces between them as even as you can.

8. Repeat this along the length of the trim. If needed, repeat along the other edge.

9. Fasten off and carefully snip the ends away.

OVER STITCH FOR FELT/FABRIC

1. This makes for a more decorative stitching effect, so use it when you want the world to see your stitches. I used this simple stitching when adding fabric and felt shapes to Bertie and Betty Bear (see Bertie and Betty Bear), to give them that hand-made look. The best stuff to use is embroidery thread in a contrasting or co-ordinating colour as it's nice and thick and will show up on your work.

2. Cut a length of thread long enough and tie a knot in one end.

3. Thread the other end onto your embroidery needle.

4. Position the trim and hold in place (you can pin it if you like).

5. Bring the needle up through the crochet and the trim and pull gently, but firmly until you reach the knot.

6. Now make an over-stitch by passing the needle over the edge of the trim and back down into the crochet.

7. In one movement, bring the needle back up again and make another stitch. You can try for even stitches, or you can vary each of them to add to that hand-crafted-with-love look.

8. Repeat this around the edge of the trim.

9. Once you're back to the beginning, make a small stitch just underneath the trim. Pass the needle through this stitch and form a loop. Bring your needle back through this loop and tighten to form a knot. Repeat this twice more to secure the thread and snip the ends carefully away.

MAKING A POM-POM

1. On fairly stiff cardboard, draw around something circular to mark the outside edge of your pom-pom and draw a smaller circle within the bigger one.

2. Cut out the donut shape and repeat, so you have two.

3. Cut long lengths of yarn and weave it evenly around the sides of the donut.

4. Keep going until you can no longer fit any more yarn through the centre.

5. With a sharp pair of scissors, cut around the outside edge of the yarn.

6. Now tie a length of yarn between the two cardboard shapes and knot tightly, securing all the yarn in place. (Leave fairly long yarn tails so that you can attach or hang the pom-pom.

7. Cut away the cardboard and trim your little pom-pom to neaten up the edges.

8. Pom-poms make great adornments for scarves, mittens, cowls and all manner of wintry accessories and are great fun to make, too.

SUPPLIERS

Lemonade Yarns www.lemonadeyarns.co.uk
The Homemakery www.thehomemakery.co.uk
Black Sheep Wools www.blacksheepwools.com
Wool Warehouse www.woolwarehouse.co.uk
Hobbycraft www.hobbycraft.co.uk
Stitch Craft Create www.stitchcraftcreate.co.uk
Jo Ann Fabric & Craft Stores www.joann.com
Hobby Lobby www.hobbylobby.com

ABOUT THE AUTHOR

Sarah is a crocheter, designer and author of the award-winning 'Annaboo's House' blog. She taught herself to crochet after giving up teaching following the birth of her second child and began writing a blog as a way of recording her progress. In her fourth year of crocheting, she now designs patterns for craft and crochet magazines, sells patterns in her Etsy shop, www.etsy.com/uk/shop/AnnaboosHouse and offers free patterns and tutorials on her blog www.annaboosbhouse.blogspot.com

THANKS

Where to begin? There have been so many people I am grateful to. First, my blog readers and social media followers who have encouraged me to crochet and have been alongside me throughout my journey. Next to the amazing people at F&W Media – to Sarah, for asking me to write this book, to Emma and Lizzy for making sense of everything I have written and to Anna for making everything look awesome. Thanks also to Jack for the beautiful photography and Kang for creating the outstanding illustrations. I also thank my friends and family for their support and encouragement to enable me to take on this huge project. Lastly, thank you to my children, Thomas and Annabelle. The best things I have ever made.

INDEX

A DAVID & CHARLES BOOK
© F&W Media International, Ltd 2015

David & Charles is an imprint of
F&W Media International, Ltd
Brunel House, Forde Close,
Newton Abbot, TQ12 4PU, UK

F&W Media International, Ltd is a
subsidiary of F+W Media, Inc
10151 Carver Road, Suite #200,
Blue Ash, OH 45242, USA

Text and Designs © Sarah Shrimpton 2015
Layout and Photography © F&W
Media International, Ltd 2015

First published in the UK and USA in 2015

Sarah Shrimpton has asserted her right
to be identified as author of this work
in accordance with the Copyright,
Designs and Patents Act, 1988.

Names of manufacturers and product
ranges are provided for the information
of readers, with no intention to
infringe copyright or trademarks.

A catalogue record for this book is
available from the British Library.

ISBN-13: 978-1-4463-0523-2 paperback
ISBN-10: 1-4463-0523-6 paperback

ISBN-13: 978-1-4463-6951-7 PDF
ISBN-10: 1-4463-6951-X PDF

ISBN-13: 978-1-4463-7257- 9 EPUB
ISBN-10: 1-4463-7257-X EPUB

Printed in USA by RR Donnelley for:
F&W Media International, Ltd
Brunel House, Forde Close,
Newton Abbot, TQ12 4PU, UK

10 9 8 7 6 5 4 3 2

Acquisitions Editor: Sarah Callard
Editor: Emma Gardner
Project Editor: Elizabeth Kingston
Pattern Checker: Lynne Rowe
Art Editor: Anna Fazakerly
Illustrator: Kuo Kang Chen
Photographer: Jack Gorman
Production Manager: Beverley Richardson

F+W Media publishes high quality
books on a wide range of subjects.
For more great book ideas visit:
www.stitchcraftcreate.co.uk

Layout of the digital edition of this
book may vary depending on reader
hardware and display settings.

31901056202452